SCRUM FOR STARTUPS

ACCELERATING GROWTH WITH AGILE PRACTICES

HARRY UNNI

ISBN
Paperback 979-8-89610-300-4
Hardcase 979-8-89673-731-5

Contents

Chapter 10   Future of Scrum in Startups   **122**

Preface

Thank you for picking up this book!

"Simplicity – the art of maximizing the amount of work not done - is essential". This is one of the 12 principles behind the agile manifesto and my favorite. It aligns perfectly with the essence of the book *The 80/20 Principle* by Richard Koch, which states that 80% of results come from 20% of efforts. For startups, the focus must be on prioritizing the most impactful tasks and cutting out anything that doesn't contribute directly to customer value. By embracing simplicity, Scrum allows startup teams to focus on what really matters, streamline processes, and deliver value swiftly, ensuring that every effort drives meaningful results and propels the company forward.

With over two decades of experience in software development and product management, I've had the privilege of leading teams across various industries, helping them embrace Agile methodologies to deliver products more efficiently and collaboratively. My journey with Agile began formally in 2011 when I first adopted Scrum practices to manage complex projects across distributed teams. Since then, I've seen firsthand how Agile principles, particularly Scrum, can transform the way teams operate, enabling them to navigate uncertainty, adapt quickly, and consistently deliver value.

Over the years, I've worked in multiple roles, including Scrum Master, Product Owner, and Agile Coach, guiding teams through challenging transformations in diverse fields such as healthcare, consumer products, and emerging technologies like AI and Augmented Reality. The more I worked with Agile teams, the clearer it became that Scrum wasn't just a framework for managing projects – it was a mindset that could empower entire organizations to innovate and grow sustainably.

One of the most defining experiences in my Agile journey came when I co-founded SMACAR Solutions, a startup specializing in Augmented Reality (AR) solutions for the retail and e-commerce sectors. At SMACAR, I led the implementation of Scrum for product development and R&D efforts, which allowed us to continuously iterate on features and meet the evolving needs of our clients. These experiences reinforced my belief in the power of Agile frameworks to drive both creativity and efficiency, especially in fast-paced startup environments.

In addition to my industry experience, I've also explored Agile principles through academic research. During my MBA, I authored the paper "Extending Technology Adoption Model by Addition of Cognitive Inhibitors", which examined the factors that hinder or facilitate technology adoption within organizations. This research provided valuable insights into how teams respond to change and adopt new processes, further shaping my approach to Agile transformations.

This book is a culmination of the lessons I've learned from both my corporate engagements and startup ventures. It is designed to be a practical guide for startups looking to harness the power of Scrum to fuel their growth, innovation, and agility. Whether you're just starting your Agile journey or refining your existing practices,

I'm confident that the strategies and insights in this book will help your team thrive.

The chapters in this book are designed to guide you through the process of implementing Scrum, scaling it as your startup grows, and overcoming common challenges that teams face.

In Chapter 1, we'll start by covering the core principles of Scrum, its origins, and its key roles, such as the Product Owner, Scrum Master, and Development Team. This chapter sets the foundation for understanding the structure of Scrum. Chapter 2 explains how to prepare your team and environment to embrace Scrum. From creating a Scrum board tailored for startups to assigning roles, this chapter will guide you in setting up your first Sprint.

Chapter 3 delves into the Sprint planning process, Daily Stand-ups, Sprint Reviews, and Retrospectives. We'll explore how to keep your team focused and deliver results incrementally. The product backlog is the backbone of Scrum. Chapter 4 covers how to create, prioritize, and refine your backlog, as well as tips for writing effective user stories. As your startup grows, scaling Scrum becomes crucial. In Chapter 5, we'll look at frameworks like Scrum of Scrums, SAFe, and LeSS, and how to coordinate multiple Scrum teams effectively.

Collaboration and communication are key to Scrum's success. Chapter 6 highlights how to build a collaborative culture and manage remote teams using Agile tools. Chapter 7 shows how to use key performance indicators (KPIs) and metrics like velocity and burndown charts to track progress and foster continuous improvement through Retrospectives. Every team faces obstacles. Chapter 8 explores strategies for addressing resistance to change, managing time and resources effectively, and handling conflicts within the team.

Chapter 9 explores a real-life example of how we successfully implemented Scrum at my startup in the deep tech space, SMACAR Solutions. This chapter shares valuable lessons and best practices from our journey. In the final Chapter 10, we'll explore emerging trends and innovations in Agile practices, and how Scrum may evolve to meet the challenges of the future startup ecosystem.

I hope this book serves as a comprehensive resource for startups looking to leverage Scrum to their advantage. As you explore each chapter, you'll gain practical insights, tools and techniques that will help your startup grow, adapt and succeed in today's competitive landscape. Happy learning!

Sincerely,

Sreehari Unnikrishnan (Harry Unni)
CSP-PO, Scrum Alliance Member

Foreword

Among the characteristics that set companies apart are their ability to innovate, pivot, and scale with unparalleled agility. A type of environment that necessitates systems and structures that are resilient as well as flexible, qualities that Scrum enumerates quite effectively. This book, *Scrum for Startups*, is a timely manual for anyone navigating the intricate waters of a startup ecosystem. It provides firsthand knowledge of how Scrum may promote productivity, teamwork, and ongoing development in any business endeavor.

It gives me great pleasure to present this book, having witnessed Sreehari's journey to becoming a proficient Agile practitioner. His experience exemplifies the transformational potential of Scrum, from taking part in our trainings to using these ideas in a fast-paced startup setting. In addition to demystifying the fundamentals of Scrum, he has created a resource that sheds light on its usefulness for startups—a distinct and useful perspective that this book deftly and thoroughly examines.

Sreehari begins by providing a solid foundation in the principles of Scrum, including its roles and ceremonies as well as its pillars of transparency, inspection, and adaption. The explanations, which are based on actual situations that demonstrate how the framework can be applied to startup issues, will be easy for readers who are unfamiliar with Scrum. This book is much more than just a primer. Actionable strategies specific to the startup ecosystem are included in each chapter, ranging from backlog management to Sprint Planning, establishing a Scrum board, and scaling Scrum as the team expands. The book also looks at methods and resources for encouraging teamwork in more prevalent remote setups, which is important knowledge for today's distributed teams.

The book's extensive use of case studies is yet another noteworthy aspect. By weaving these real-world examples throughout, Sreehari brings the theoretical concepts of Scrum into clear, practical focus. Readers will acquire a sophisticated grasp of how Scrum may be used by startups to set priorities, preserve flexibility in the face of expansion, and optimize workflows for optimal output. A thorough examination of a startup's Scrum journey is provided via the inclusion of SMACAR Solutions, a complete case study that describes obstacles, adjustments, and quantifiable achievements.

The book also offers a forward-looking perspective on the future of Scrum in the startup ecosystem. Trends in Agile practices, including AI-driven Scrum enhancements, are explored, setting the stage for how Scrum will continue to evolve and empower startups in the years to come.

Having a system that promotes organized innovation is crucial as the business landscape grows more competitive. Scrum not only satisfies that but also perfectly complements the ethos of entrepreneurship by fostering flexibility, resiliency, and quick learning. By presenting Scrum through the lens of startup challenges and opportunities, *Scrum for Startups* serves as both a handbook and a guide. I am confident this book will be an asset for startup founders, team leads, and innovators seeking to harness Agile practices to drive growth and achieve lasting success.

Hemanth Kumar,
CPO, Leanpitch Technologies Pvt. Ltd.

Introduction

"Our highest priority is to satisfy the customer through early and continuous delivery of valuable software."

The Startup Challenge

Imagine this: You're the founder of a fast-growing startup. What started as a small team of passionate innovators working on a unique solution is now a full-fledged company with customers, investors, and high expectations. But as your company grows, so do the challenges. Suddenly, the lean and agile nature that made your startup thrive is being weighed down by communication breakdowns, missed deadlines, and unclear priorities.

One week, your team is focused on building a new product feature. The next, you're scrambling to fix bugs and address customer complaints. The pressure is mounting, your team is burning out, and you're losing sight of the big picture. You realize you need a structured approach—but one that still allows for flexibility and fast iteration. This is where Scrum comes in.

The Need for Agility in Startups

Startups face a unique set of challenges: limited resources, rapid growth, high uncertainty, and a constant demand for innovation. Traditional project management methods often fall short in these environments as they rely on predictability and long-term planning—luxuries that most startups simply don't have. What startups need is a framework that allows them to adapt quickly, pivot when necessary, and stay focused on delivering value to customers.

Scrum, an Agile project management framework, offers exactly that. It provides the structure needed to manage complex projects while maintaining the flexibility that startups require to stay competitive.

As startups strive to build valuable solutions, they face four key risks: **value risk, usability risk, feasibility risk**, and **business viability risk**.

- **Value Risk**: Are we building something customers actually want?

- **Usability Risk**: Will users be able to use the product effectively?

- **Feasibility Risk**: Can we build the solution with the technology and resources we have?

- **Business Viability Risk**: Is the product aligned with the business model?

Agile frameworks like Scrum are designed to mitigate these risks by breaking down work into manageable sprints, emphasizing collaboration, and continuously incorporating feedback. Scrum helps startups streamline their processes, improve team dynamics, and deliver high-quality products at speed.

The Evolution of Scrum

Scrum's origins can be traced back to a 1986 paper titled "The New New Product Development Game" by Hirotaka Takeuchi and Ikujiro Nonaka, published in the *Harvard Business Review*. The authors introduced a flexible, iterative and collaborative approach to product development, inspired by rugby, where the team works together to move the ball down the field.

In the early 1990s, Ken Schwaber and Jeff Sutherland formalized Scrum as a framework for software development, building on Takeuchi and Nonaka's ideas. Scrum made its first public appearance at the OOPSLA conference in 1995, and since then, it has evolved through continuous improvements, largely guided by the publication of the *Scrum Guide*.

Key Milestones in Scrum's Evolution:

- **1986**: Takeuchi and Nonaka publish "The New New Product Development Game."

- **1993**: Jeff Sutherland and his team adapt Scrum for software development.

- **1995**: Ken Schwaber and Jeff Sutherland present Scrum at the OOPSLA conference.

- **2001**: The *Agile Manifesto* is published, with Scrum as one of its key frameworks.

- **2010**: The first official version of the *Scrum Guide* is released.

- **2020**: The latest version of the *Scrum Guide* is published, reflecting the ongoing evolution of Scrum practices.

Scrum in the Industry Today

What started as a framework for software development has now been widely adopted across various industries – finance, healthcare, education, and more. Scrum's versatility and adaptability make it the go-to solution for managing complex projects in environments that require flexibility and speed.

Here are some key statistics to highlight its effectiveness:

- **87%** of Agile-focused organizations use Scrum.

- **66%** of Agile businesses utilize the Scrum framework.

- Teams that adopt Scrum effectively have reported productivity improvements of **300% to 400%**.

- **78%** of Scrum users recommend the framework to others, making it a widely trusted tool for driving growth.

Success Rates and Industry Endorsements

Scrum has also led to significantly higher success rates in projects:

- Projects managed with Agile methodologies, including Scrum, report a success rate of **75%**, compared to **56%** for traditional project management methods.

Here are some quotes from industry leaders:

"Scrum is not a methodology. It's a framework for discovering what works in your unique context."
— Ken Schwaber

"Agility is not about doing more with less, but about doing the right things at the right time, with just the right amount of effort."
— Mike Cohn

"The beauty of Scrum is that it allows you to continuously inspect and adapt, keeping your team on the path to success."
— Jeff Sutherland

"If you adopt only one Agile practice, let it be Retrospectives. Everything else will follow."
— Woody Zuill

"Scrum is a tool to uncover better ways of working—not just to get faster but to get smarter."
— Henrik Kniberg

Why This Book?

Scrum for Startups: Accelerating Growth with Agile Practices is written specifically for startup founders, Agile practitioners, and working professionals who want to harness the power of Scrum to accelerate growth and drive innovation.

Whether you're familiar with Scrum or just starting to explore Agile methodologies, this book will provide you with actionable insights and real-world examples that you can apply directly to your startup environment. You will learn how to implement Scrum from the ground up, set up your first sprints, manage your Product Backlog, and overcome the common challenges that startups face when scaling their teams and products.

By the end of this book, you'll understand:

- How to set up Scrum in your startup, even if your team is new to Agile practices.

- How to structure and execute sprints to deliver value faster.

- How to scale Scrum as your startup grows, ensuring that your teams stay aligned and productive.

- How to measure success using key performance indicators (KPIs) and drive continuous improvement.

- How to leverage Scrum to foster innovation and maintain a competitive edge in a fast-paced market.

A Clear Path Forward

This book is designed to be more than just a theoretical guide. It's a practical, step-by-step playbook that will help you turn the principles of Scrum into tangible results for your business. Whether you're struggling to manage rapid growth, improve team communication, or deliver products that meet your customers' needs, Scrum offers a solution.

By adopting the practices outlined in this book, you'll not only streamline your processes but also create a culture of continuous improvement within your startup. This will allow you to remain agile, adapt to changes quickly, and stay focused on what really matters: delivering value to your customers.

Chapter 1

Understanding Scrum Basics

"Welcome changing requirements, even late in development. Agile processes harness change for the customer's competitive advantage."

What is Scrum?

Scrum is an Agile framework designed to help teams address complex, adaptive problems by delivering incremental, tangible results. It focuses on iterative progress through regular feedback loops and the flexibility to change course as needed. While Scrum is commonly used in software development, its principles can be applied to a wide variety of industries, from healthcare to manufacturing, marketing, and more.

The essence of Scrum is collaboration—teams work in close coordination, iterating on tasks and delivering value at regular intervals, typically every 1 to 4 weeks. Each cycle, known as a **Sprint**, ends with a working increment of the product, which can be evaluated and adjusted based on feedback.

The Pillars of Empiricism: Transparency, Inspection, and Adaptation

At its core, Scrum is built on the principle of **empiricism**. Empiricism emphasizes that knowledge comes from experience, and decisions should be based on observation and evidence rather than speculation. The three pillars that uphold empiricism in Scrum are:

1. **Transparency**: Ensures that all aspects of the Scrum process are visible to everyone involved.

2. **Inspection**: Encourages regular inspection of both the product and process.

3. **Adaptation**: Teams adapt their processes and goals based on the feedback they receive during inspection.

The Agile Manifesto: A Shift in Thinking

The **Agile Manifesto** was born out of frustration with the rigid, inflexible nature of traditional project management methodologies like Waterfall. Prior to 2001, the software industry faced constant struggles with meeting deadlines, adapting to changes, and delivering value that matched customer expectations. Projects would often take years to complete, and by the time they were delivered, they no longer fully met the business needs.

In response to these challenges, 17 software developers and thought leaders met in 2001 to create the Agile Manifesto.

The manifesto promotes a more adaptive, flexible way of working, emphasizing collaboration and continuous delivery of value. Though initially designed for software development, the manifesto's values and principles have been adopted across industries worldwide.

The **four key values** of the Agile Manifesto are:

1. **Individuals and interactions** over processes and tools.

2. **Working software** over comprehensive documentation.

3. **Customer collaboration** over contract negotiation.

4. **Responding to change** over following a plan.

These values prioritize flexibility, collaboration, and responsiveness to change. Companies like **Spotify** have built their organizational culture around Agile, allowing them to remain competitive and innovative in the fast-paced music streaming industry. Similarly, **ING**, a major financial institution, restructured its entire organization to embrace Agile, improving time-to-market and internal collaboration.

The 12 Principles Behind the Agile Manifesto

The Agile Manifesto is supported by **12 guiding principles** that shape how Agile teams operate. These principles emphasize continuous delivery, collaboration, and adaptability:

1. Our highest priority is to satisfy the customer through early and continuous delivery of valuable software.

2. Welcome changing requirements, even late in development. Agile processes harness change for the customer's competitive advantage.

3. Deliver working software frequently, from a couple of weeks to a couple of months, with a preference for the shorter timescale.

4. Business people and developers must work together daily throughout the project.

5. Build projects around motivated individuals. Give them the environment and support they need, and trust them to get the job done.

6. The most efficient and effective method of conveying information to and within a development team is face-to-face conversation.

7. Working software is the primary measure of progress.

8. Agile processes promote sustainable development. The sponsors, developers, and users should be able to maintain a constant pace indefinitely.

9. Continuous attention to technical excellence and good design enhances agility.

10. Simplicity—the art of maximizing the amount of work not done—is essential.

11. The best architectures, requirements, and designs emerge from self-organizing teams.

12. At regular intervals, the team reflects on how to become more effective, then tunes and adjusts its behavior accordingly.

These principles guide Agile teams to focus on delivering value early and often, welcoming changes and ensuring customer satisfaction.

The Key Roles in Scrum

Scrum assigns specific responsibilities to key roles that ensure focus, accountability and continuous improvement:

1. **Product Owner**: The Product Owner is the voice of the customer and holds the vision for the product. Their primary job is to manage the **Product Backlog**—a prioritized list of tasks and features. The Product Owner interacts with stakeholders to gather input and ensure the team focuses on the highest-value items.

2. **Scrum Master**: Often referred to as the "servant leader," the Scrum Master facilitates the Scrum process. They ensure that the team adheres to Scrum values and practices and help eliminate obstacles.

3. **Development Team**: This cross-functional group has the necessary skills to deliver a working product. The team is self-organizing, meaning they decide how to execute the tasks during a sprint.

The Scrum Framework

Scrum is built around a set of regular **events** that ensure alignment and progress toward a common goal. These events create opportunities for inspection and adaptation, which are essential to the empirical approach Scrum is founded on:

1. **Sprints**: A **Sprint** is a time-boxed iteration where the Scrum Team works on a specific set of tasks to deliver a potentially shippable product increment. The duration of each sprint is fixed, usually between 1 and 4 weeks.

2. **Sprint Planning**: During Sprint Planning, the team collaborates with the Product Owner to select high-priority tasks from the Product Backlog and define the sprint goal.

3. **Daily Scrum**: Also known as the **Daily Stand-up**, this is a short meeting where the team discusses what was done yesterday, what will be done today, and any obstacles.

4. **Sprint Review**: At the end of the sprint, the team presents their completed work to stakeholders for feedback. This helps ensure the product is on track.

5. **Sprint Retrospective**: After the Sprint Review, the team conducts a retrospective to reflect on what went well, what didn't, and how they can improve.

Key Scrum Artifacts

Scrum relies on a set of **artifacts** that help the team remain transparent and focused on their progress. These artifacts are crucial in managing work and ensuring that the team consistently delivers value.

1. **Product Backlog**: The Product Backlog is an ordered list of everything that might be needed in the product. Managed by the Product Owner, it evolves continuously as new information emerges. Items in the backlog are typically user stories or features that add value to the product.

   Tip: Keep the Product Backlog refined. Regularly grooming the backlog ensures that items are well-defined, relevant, and prioritized, which helps avoid scope creep.

2. **Sprint Backlog**: The Sprint Backlog consists of selected Product Backlog Items that the team commits to completing during the sprint. It provides transparency by showing what the team is working on and how they plan to achieve the sprint goal.

3. **Increment**: The Increment is the sum of all the Product Backlog Items completed during the sprint. It represents progress toward the final product and must meet the **Definition of Done** before it can be considered releasable.

   Tip: Ensure that the Definition of Done is clearly defined and consistently applied. This prevents confusion about what constitutes a "completed" task and ensures high-quality output.

Core Values in Scrum

Source: https://www.scrum.org/resources/blog/5-scrum-values-take-center-stage

The Scrum pillars of transparency, inspection, and adaptation come to life and build trust for everyone when these core values are embodied and lived by the Scrum team. The Scrum team members learn and explore these values as they work with the Scrum events, roles, and artifacts.

Case Study: Transition from Waterfall to Scrum

One company that successfully transitioned from the traditional Waterfall methodology to Scrum was **HealthTech**, a healthcare software provider.

HealthTech initially followed a Waterfall approach, where the development process was linear and tasks were completed sequentially. This led to long development cycles, delays, and costly rework when customer needs changed midway through the project. By the time the product was delivered, it often didn't fully meet the business needs.

When the leadership at HealthTech realized the inefficiencies of Waterfall, they decided to switch to Scrum in 2015. They started with a small pilot team to test the framework. However, the transition wasn't easy – initially, there was resistance from the development teams, who were used to the predictability of Waterfall. Stakeholders were skeptical about delivering working increments every few weeks.

After a few sprints, the teams started seeing improvements. For example:

- **Improved Flexibility**: Scrum allowed HealthTech to adjust priorities based on customer feedback, which was crucial in the healthcare industry where regulations and customer needs shift frequently.

- **Faster Time-to-Market**: The company was able to release smaller increments of the product sooner, enabling them to test features with real users and gather feedback early on.

- **Increased Collaboration**: Daily Stand-ups and Retrospectives fostered better communication, particularly between developers, product managers, and compliance teams.

Over the next year, HealthTech fully embraced Scrum and scaled it across departments. As a result, they reported a **30% reduction in development time** and a **40% increase in customer**

satisfaction due to their ability to deliver features that aligned more closely with user needs.

HealthTech's journey is a testament to how Scrum can drive transformation, even in highly regulated and complex industries like healthcare.

Key Takeaways

- Scrum is an Agile framework designed to help teams tackle complex problems by delivering value incrementally and adapting to feedback.

- Empiricism is at the heart of Scrum, relying on transparency, inspection, and adaptation to guide decision-making and process improvement.

- The Agile Manifesto shifted thinking away from rigid project management practices, emphasizing flexibility, collaboration, and delivering continuous value.

- The 12 Principles of Agile emphasize the importance of customer collaboration, adapting to change, and maintaining a sustainable development pace.

- Scrum values of commitment, focus, openness, respect, and courage guide the behavior of the team, fostering trust and accountability.

- Scrum teams consist of key roles: Product Owner, Scrum Master, and Development Team, each with specific responsibilities that ensure accountability and continuous improvement.

- The Scrum Framework revolves around regular events like Sprints, Daily Stand-ups, Sprint Reviews, and Retrospectives, which keep the team aligned and focused.

- Scrum Artifacts, such as the Product Backlog, Sprint Backlog, and Increment, provide transparency and help teams manage progress toward the product goal.

- A successful transition to Scrum, as seen in case studies like HealthTech, can lead to improved flexibility, faster time-to-market, and better collaboration across teams.

Chapter 2

Setting Up Scrum in a Startup

"Deliver working software frequently, from a couple of weeks to a couple of months, with a preference for the shorter timescale."

Preparing the Team and Environment

When introducing Scrum into a startup, the first step is preparing both the team and the work environment to support Agile practices. Startups are often dynamic, with a small number of employees wearing multiple hats. This makes Scrum's structured yet flexible approach particularly valuable, but it also requires proper groundwork.

1. **Cultivating the Right Mindset:**

    - Building a mindset that embraces change is crucial in a startup, where team members are used to tackling many tasks and decisions simultaneously. Scrum's iterative nature can feel slow to those who are used to tackling multiple problems at once. It's important to explain that while Scrum introduces structure, it's designed to help the team focus and deliver higher quality work more frequently.

- **Example**: A SaaS startup might initially find it challenging to shift from a chaotic, reactive development process to Scrum's planned sprints. By emphasizing how the method will lead to faster, more manageable development cycles, the team can begin to see the long-term benefits.

- **Tip**: Regular check-ins are vital. Hold one-on-one meetings with key team members to address any concerns or misconceptions about Scrum and discuss how it will fit into their day-to-day responsibilities.

2. **Securing Buy-in from Leadership**:

- Leadership support is critical to the success of Scrum. Founders, managers, and investors in a startup often demand fast results, which can create pressure to revert to old habits if immediate outcomes aren't visible. Leaders must commit to Scrum for the long term and allow time for teams to adapt to the new process.

- **Example**: At **Buffer**, a social media management startup, the leadership team initially struggled to see the benefits of Scrum as they were used to focusing on quick releases to stay competitive. However, after allowing the team to adjust and implement a few sprints, they noticed the improved consistency in product delivery, which positively impacted the customer experience.

- **Tip**: Hold a dedicated leadership workshop that explains Scrum's long-term benefits—faster pivots, increased customer satisfaction, and fewer last-minute crises.

3. **Choosing the Right Tools**:

- For startups, the choice of tools can be overwhelming. While tools like **Trello**, **Jira**, or **Monday.com** are popular, it's important to select a tool that suits the current team size and needs.

- **Example**: A three-person startup might start with a physical whiteboard and sticky notes to manage tasks during their first few sprints. Once the team grows, they can migrate to a more complex digital tool like Jira, which allows for detailed tracking and reporting.

- **Tip**: Conduct a trial period with different tools. Let the team test each tool for one sprint and choose the one that feels most natural.

Introducing Scrum to the Team

Bringing Scrum into a startup can feel like a big change, especially if the team is used to a less structured way of working. The transition needs to be smooth and supportive to ensure success.

1. **Conducting a Scrum Workshop**:

- Introducing Scrum in a structured, hands-on way will help the team understand how it will impact their workflow. A half-day workshop can go a long way in demystifying Scrum.

- **Tip**: Use real projects as examples during the workshop. Ask the team to bring in tasks they are currently working on, and together, break them down into smaller, sprint-sized items. This provides immediate context and makes Scrum more approachable.

2. Clarifying Roles:

- In startups, roles often overlap. It's not uncommon for developers to take on project management responsibilities or for marketing leads to contribute to product development. In Scrum, these blurred lines can cause confusion unless clearly defined.

- **Example**: In a FinTech startup with only five employees, the CTO might initially take on the role of both Product Owner and Scrum Master. This is acceptable in the early stages, but it's important to eventually define and separate these roles as the company grows.

- **Tip**: Provide role-specific training. A Product Owner training session could focus on backlog prioritization and stakeholder communication, while a Scrum Master session could address how to facilitate effective Retrospectives and manage conflicts.

3. Managing Resistance to Change:

- Change is hard for any team, especially when introducing a new way of working like Scrum. Resistance may come in the form of passive reluctance, where team members go through the motions but don't fully commit to the process.

- **Example**: At **Shopify**, when Scrum was first introduced, developers were initially resistant to attending Daily Stand-ups, viewing them as unnecessary interruptions. The Scrum Master addressed this by shortening the stand-ups and focusing on actionable updates, which eventually won over the team.

- **Tip**: Acknowledge resistance and address it head-on. Regularly collect feedback through anonymous surveys to see how the team feels about Scrum after the first few sprints. Address concerns during Retrospectives to continually refine the process.

Creating a Scrum Board Tailored for Startups

The **Scrum board** is a visual representation of the team's workflow and is critical in making tasks visible and trackable.

1. **Setting Up the Basic Columns**:

   - The traditional Scrum board includes three basic columns: **To Do**, **In Progress**, and **Done**. In a startup, however, you might need to customize it further to reflect your specific workflow.

   - **Example**: A **D2C e-commerce startup** might add an extra column for "**Waiting for Approval**" to track tasks that require stakeholder or legal approval before they can be considered complete.

   - **Tip**: Keep your board simple at the start, especially for smaller teams. Only add additional columns as needed, such as "Blocked" for tasks that are stuck or "Review" for items that need testing or stakeholder sign-off.

2. **Customizing for Your Startup**:

   - Startups often have unique needs, and the Scrum board can be adapted to reflect this. For example, a startup focused on hardware development might include phases like

Prototyping and **Testing** on their board, while a content-focused startup may add stages like **Drafting** and **Editing**.

- **Tip**: Revisit and refine your board regularly. The board you set up on day one might not be the same as the one you use three months in, as your team's needs evolve. Use Retrospectives to assess if the board needs adjustments.

3. **Choosing Digital or Physical Boards**:

- While digital boards like **Jira** and **Trello** offer flexibility for remote teams, physical boards are highly effective for small, co-located teams. Startups that work out of shared spaces often benefit from the visibility and collaboration that a physical board brings.

- **Example**: **InVision**, a fully remote design software company, uses digital Scrum boards to manage sprints across different time zones. On the other hand, a local food delivery startup might use a physical board to allow all employees to see updates at a glance in their shared workspace.

- **Tip**: If your team is hybrid, consider using both. Physical boards can complement digital boards by keeping the most critical tasks visible, even when working remotely.

Difference Between a Project Manager and a Scrum Master

Aspect	Project Manager	Scrum Master
Role	Directs and controls the project, focusing on scope, timelines, budget and resources.	Facilitates the Scrum process and helps the team self-organize and remove impediments.
Decision-Making	Central decision-maker for the project; assigns tasks and manages deadlines.	Facilitates team decision-making but does not make decisions for the team.
Focus	Delivers the project on time and within budget, adhering to a predetermined plan.	Ensures that the team follows Scrum principles and continuously improves.
Responsibilities	Plans project tasks, assigns work, monitors progress and reports to upper management.	Coaches the team on Agile practices, removes obstacles and fosters collaboration.

Aspect	Project Manager	Scrum Master
Team Empower-ment	Often follows a top-down approach where the manager directs the team.	Uses a bottom-up approach, empowering the team to be self-sufficient and self-organized.
Success Measurement	Success is measured by meeting deadlines, staying within scope and budget.	Success is measured by the team's ability to adapt, collaborate and deliver value through continuous improvement.

Why the Scrum Master Role Matters

The Scrum Master's role is critical because it shifts the focus from managing people and tasks to facilitating a process where the team can self-organize, solve problems, and continuously improve. By removing obstacles and fostering a culture of collaboration, the Scrum Master helps the team become more autonomous, which in turn enables faster delivery of value and greater adaptability in a dynamic startup environment. This role encourages innovation and allows the team to remain flexible in the face of changing market conditions, which is essential for the long-term success of a Scrum-based startup.

Case Study: A Startup Team Setting Up Their First Scrum Board

Let's take the example of **TechFit**, a fitness-tech startup developing a mobile app for at-home workouts. The company's team consists of six members: two developers, one designer, one product manager, a marketing specialist, and a co-founder.

Step 1: Assigning Roles

- **Product Owner**: Sarah, the co-founder, takes on the role of Product Owner due to her deep understanding of customer needs and business goals.

- **Scrum Master**: The product manager, John, takes on the Scrum Master role. His main responsibilities are facilitating the Scrum process and removing any obstacles that slow the team down.

- **Development Team**: The two developers and the designer form the cross-functional development team, handling all technical aspects of building the app.

Step 2: Setting Up the Scrum Board

- The team chooses to use a digital Scrum board on **Trello** for remote accessibility. They set up basic columns: **To Do**, **In Progress**, **Testing**, and **Done**. They add color-coded labels for priority levels (e.g., critical bugs, minor improvements).

- The board includes specific tasks from the Product Backlog, such as "Integrate video workouts," "Design user dashboard," and "Fix bugs in workout tracker."

Step 3: Sprint Planning

- During their first **Sprint Planning** session, Sarah identifies the highest-priority tasks: integrating the video workout feature and designing the user dashboard.

- The development team discusses each task, estimating that they can complete the video feature within the two-week sprint, but the user dashboard might extend into the next sprint.

Step 4: Daily Scrums

- Each morning, the team holds a quick 15-minute **Daily Scrum** via video call. One of the developers mentions a bug with the video streaming. They move the task to the **In Progress** column and assign it to the developer who raised the issue.

Step 5: Sprint Review and Retrospective

- At the end of the sprint, the team demonstrates the integrated video workout feature to Sarah. During the **Sprint Retrospective**, the team reflects on what went well (good collaboration) and what needs improvement (better time estimation).

After three sprints, the team feels confident about its Scrum process and continues refining its board and roles, adapting to its evolving needs.

Key Takeaways

- Preparing the team and environment is crucial when introducing Scrum to a startup. A mindset shift toward iterative work and embracing change helps teams transition smoothly.

- Leadership support is vital to Scrum's success. Buy-in from founders and investors ensures the team has time to adapt and consistently follow Scrum practices.

- Selecting the right tools, whether physical or digital, is key to managing tasks. Start with simple tools like a whiteboard or sticky notes for smaller teams and move to digital solutions like Trello or Jira as the team grows.

- Conducting a Scrum workshop is an effective way to introduce the framework to the team and ensure a smooth transition. Using real projects as examples helps clarify the process.

- Clearly defining Scrum roles (Product Owner, Scrum Master, Development Team) helps prevent role overlap, which is common in small startups where employees wear multiple hats.

- Addressing resistance to change is essential. Regular feedback and Retrospectives help identify concerns early and refine the process to suit the team's evolving needs.

- A tailored Scrum board is important for startups. Whether physical or digital, the board must reflect the team's unique workflow, with room for refinement as the team grows.

- The role of the Scrum Master is critical in guiding the team's self-organization and ensuring continuous improvement, which is vital in the dynamic startup environment.

- Scrum fosters flexibility and collaboration, helping startups manage complexity and deliver value efficiently, even with limited resources.

Chapter 3

Planning and Executing Sprints

❊

"Business people and developers must work together
daily throughout the project."

Introduction to Sprints

A **sprint** is the heart of the Scrum process – a fixed-length, iterative cycle where teams work on a set of prioritized tasks to deliver a working product increment. Sprints typically last between one and four weeks, with two weeks being a common duration for many startups. Each sprint should have a clear goal, specific deliverables, and end with a potentially shippable product increment.

For startups, executing sprints effectively can be the difference between rapid, agile development and falling into the trap of disorganized chaos. In this chapter, we'll explore the mechanics of **Sprint Planning**, **Daily Stand-ups**, and **Sprint Reviews and Retrospectives**, while providing a real-world example of a startup planning a two-week sprint to develop a new feature.

Scrum Process Flow Diagram

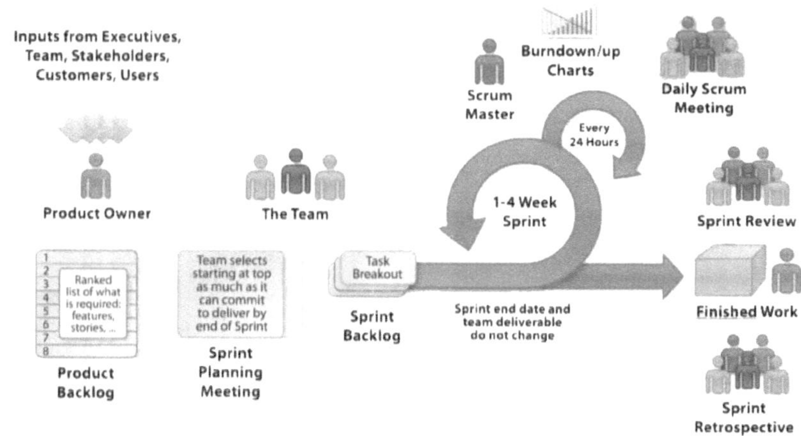

Source: https://www.cleanpng.com/png-scrum-agile-software-development-kanban-computer-s-804958

Sprint Planning and Goal Setting

Sprint planning is one of the most important events in the Scrum framework. It sets the foundation for what the team will accomplish in the upcoming sprint. During this event, the **Product Owner**, **Scrum Master**, and the **Development Team** collaborate to define the sprint goal and select tasks from the **Product Backlog** to focus on during the sprint.

Step 1: Defining the Sprint Goal

The **sprint goal** is a high-level objective that the team should achieve by the end of the sprint. It's not about completing every task in the Sprint Backlog but ensuring that the most important goal is met. This goal acts as a north star, guiding the team's efforts throughout the sprint.

- **Example**: In a **FinTech startup**, the sprint goal might be to integrate a new feature that allows users to schedule automatic transfers between bank accounts. While there may be several smaller tasks involved (designing the user interface, back-end integration, testing), the overall goal is focused on delivering that new feature.

Best Practice Tip: Keep sprint goals focused and achievable. Trying to pack too many tasks or objectives into a single sprint can lead to burnout and missed deadlines.

Step 2: Selecting Tasks from the Product Backlog

Once the sprint goal is set, the **Development Team** works with the **Product Owner** to select items from the **Product Backlog** that contribute to achieving that goal. These tasks are moved into the **Sprint Backlog**. The team estimates the effort required for each task and prioritizes them based on importance and complexity.

- **Example**: Continuing with the FinTech example, the team might break down the automatic transfer feature into tasks like "create UI mockups," "set up transfer scheduling API," "develop backend logic for transaction handling," and "write automated tests for the feature."

During this stage, the team should be realistic about its capacity. Overcommitting during Sprint Planning is a common pitfall, especially for startups where resources are limited, and priorities can change rapidly.

Step 3: Estimating Task Effort

Estimating the effort required for each task can be challenging, especially if the team is new to Scrum. Common estimation techniques include **story points** (based on complexity and effort) or **time-based estimates** (e.g. hours or days).

- **Tip**: Encourage the team to use relative estimation (e.g., "task A is twice as complex as task B") to avoid getting bogged down in trying to assign exact hours. The goal is to focus on the relative effort required to complete each task, not to create a perfectly accurate estimate.

Step 4: Creating the Sprint Backlog

The **Sprint Backlog** is the list of tasks the team commits to completing during the sprint. These tasks should all contribute to achieving the sprint goal, and once they are moved to the **Done** column, the product increment should be ready to ship.

- **Best Practice**: Ensure that every task in the Sprint Backlog has a clear **Definition of Done**. This prevents confusion about when a task is truly complete. For example, in the FinTech startup, the Definition of Done might include "UI is user-tested and meets accessibility standards" or "code passes all automated tests and is deployed to staging."

Conducting Daily Stand-ups

The **Daily Scrum** or **Daily Stand-up** is a quick 15-minute meeting where the team gathers to discuss progress, plan for the day, and identify any roadblocks. The purpose of the stand-up is to ensure the team stays aligned and to surface any issues early.

Structure of a Daily Stand-up

Each team member answers three questions:

1. **What did you do yesterday?**

2. **What will you do today?**

3. **Are there any blockers or impediments?**

   - **Example**: In the Daily Stand-up for our FinTech startup, one developer might say, "Yesterday, I completed the UI mockups. Today, I'm starting the back-end integration for the transfer scheduling feature. The only blocker is waiting for API documentation from the banking partner."

The stand-up is not a status meeting for managers. Its purpose is to help the team coordinate and share information. The **Scrum Master** should ensure that the meeting stays focused and does not deviate into long discussions or problem-solving sessions. If any detailed issues arise, they should be addressed after the stand-up with the relevant team members.

Holding Sprint Reviews and Retrospectives

At the end of each sprint, the team holds two important meetings: the **Sprint Review** and the **Sprint Retrospective**.

Sprint Review

The **Sprint Review** is a meeting where the team presents the completed work to stakeholders for feedback. This is an opportunity to showcase the product increment and gather input on what has been achieved. It's important to note that the Sprint Review is not just a demo – it's a collaborative meeting where the team discusses what was accomplished, what is coming next, and how well the team is progressing toward the overall product goal.

- **Example**: In the FinTech startup, the team demonstrates the automatic transfer feature to stakeholders, including product managers and customer support teams. Stakeholders might provide feedback on the user interface or suggest additional use cases that the team hadn't considered during Sprint Planning.

Best Practice: Use the feedback gathered during the Sprint Review to inform the next sprint. If stakeholders identify a critical issue or opportunity, the team can prioritize it in the next Sprint Planning session.

Sprint Retrospective

The **Sprint Retrospective** is an internal meeting where the Scrum team reflects on the sprint and identifies areas for improvement. The goal of the retrospective is continuous improvement – how can the team work better in the next sprint?

- **Structure of the Retrospective**:

  - **What went well?** (Celebrate successes)

  - **What didn't go well?** (Identify pain points)

  - **What can we improve?** (Actionable steps for the next sprint)

- **Example**: In the FinTech startup retrospective, the team might acknowledge that the back-end integration took longer than expected because of unforeseen technical challenges. Moving forward, they decide to allocate more time to researching third-party APIs in future sprints.

Best Practice Tip: Retrospectives should always result in a concrete action plan. If the team identifies an area for improvement, make sure there's a clear owner and timeline for implementing the change. This ensures the retrospective leads to real improvements, not just discussions.

Recommended Duration for Scrum Ceremonies Based on Sprint Length:

Sprint Ceremony	1 Week Sprint	2 Week Sprint	3 Week Sprint	4 Week Sprint
Sprint Planning	1-2 hours	2-4 hours	3-6 hours	4-8 hours
Daily Stand-up	15 minutes	15 minutes	15 minutes	15 minutes
Sprint Review	30-60 minutes	1-2 hours	1.5-3 hours	2-4 hours
Sprint Retrospective	30-45 minutes	1-1.5 hours	1-2 hours	1.5-3 hours

Key Notes:

- Sprint Planning: This is typically longer, as it's where the team discusses what work will be done and how they will achieve the Sprint Goal. The time increases with the Sprint length to allow for adequate planning.

- Daily Stand-up: This meeting remains constant at 15 minutes regardless of Sprint length, as it's a brief check-in focused on updates and blockers.

- Sprint Review: The time allotted for the Sprint Review increases with Sprint length, allowing for a more thorough demonstration of completed work and stakeholder feedback.

- Sprint Retrospective: Like the Sprint Review, the Retrospective's duration grows with the Sprint length, allowing for a deeper reflection on what went well and what can be improved.

Case Study: A Startup Planning a Two-Week Sprint to Develop a New Feature

Let's take the example of **ShopEase**, a startup building a shopping app that helps users find the best deals on groceries. The team consists of a Product Owner (Sarah), a Scrum Master (Alex), and a development team of five people (two developers, a designer, a QA tester, and a marketing specialist).

Sprint Planning: Defining the Sprint Goal

For their upcoming two-week sprint, the sprint goal is to develop a new feature that alerts users when their favorite items go on sale. The team breaks this goal down into specific tasks:

- **Design notification templates for sale alerts**

- **Implement sale alert feature in the mobile app**

- **Test sale alert notifications**

Sarah, the Product Owner, works closely with the team to prioritize these tasks based on customer feedback and market demand.

Daily Stand-ups: Managing Progress and Challenges

During the Daily Stand-ups, Alex, the Scrum Master, ensures that the team stays aligned. On Day four of the sprint, one of the developers mentions that the notification system is causing performance issues. The Scrum Master suggests the developer work closely with the QA tester to identify potential optimizations.

Sprint Review: Gathering Feedback from Stakeholders

At the Sprint Review, the team demonstrates the sale alert feature. While the core functionality works as expected, one of the marketing stakeholders suggests adding a feature to allow users to customize the types of alerts they receive. The team agrees to explore this in the next sprint.

Sprint Retrospective: Continuous Improvement

During the Sprint Retrospective, the team reflects on what worked well and what could be improved. They acknowledge that testing could have started earlier in the sprint to catch performance issues sooner. For the next sprint, the team decides to integrate testing more thoroughly into their process by conducting mid-sprint QA checks.

Key Takeaways

- Sprints are the core of Scrum, with fixed-length iterations (typically 1-4 weeks) aimed at delivering a potentially shippable product increment.

- Sprint Planning sets the foundation for the sprint, with the team collaboratively defining the Sprint Goal and selecting tasks from the Product Backlog that align with that goal.

- Sprint Goals should be focused and achievable, guiding the team's work and ensuring the most important objective is met by the end of the sprint.

- Daily Stand-ups help the team stay aligned, with each member sharing what they've done, what they plan to do, and any blockers they face.

- Sprint Reviews allow teams to showcase completed work to stakeholders, gather feedback, and adjust the product backlog based on that feedback.

- Sprint Retrospectives are crucial for continuous improvement, where teams reflect on what went well, what didn't, and how to improve in the next sprint.

- Estimating effort during Sprint Planning helps teams manage their capacity and avoid overcommitting, a common pitfall in startups.

- Clear Definitions of Done ensure that completed tasks meet quality standards and are ready to be shipped or deployed.

- The timing of Scrum ceremonies—planning, stand-ups, reviews, and retrospectives—should be adjusted based on the sprint length, with longer sprints requiring more time for planning and reflection.

- Real-world sprint execution, like in the case of ShopEase, illustrates how Scrum helps startups stay agile, adjust based on feedback, and continuously improve through focused, iterative work.

Chapter 4

Product Backlog Management

"Build projects around motivated individuals.
Give them the environment and support they need,
and trust them to get the job done."

The **Product Backlog** is the backbone of Scrum's planning process. It is an ordered list of everything that might be needed for the product, serving as the single source of truth for what the team will work on next. Unlike traditional project management where all tasks are planned upfront, the Product Backlog is dynamic and evolves based on feedback, new ideas, and shifting priorities. For startups, managing and refining the backlog efficiently can be the difference between building a product that meets customer needs and wasting valuable resources on low-priority features.

This chapter explores the key aspects of managing the product backlog, including **creating and prioritizing the backlog**, **writing effective user stories**, and **managing and refining the backlog**.

Creating and Prioritizing the Product Backlog

The **Product Backlog** is a prioritized list of product features, enhancements, bug fixes, technical debt, and other tasks that need to be completed. It is maintained by the **Product Owner** and is continuously updated based on feedback from stakeholders and the development team.

Step 1: Defining the Product Vision

Before creating the backlog, it's essential to define a clear **product vision**. The product vision serves as the guiding light, helping the team stay aligned on what they are building and why. Without a solid vision, the backlog can become an unorganized list of tasks with no clear direction.

- **Example**: In a startup developing an app for online tutoring, the product vision could be "to provide seamless virtual learning experiences that connect students with expert tutors worldwide." This vision should be front and center when creating backlog items to ensure each task contributes to the overall goal.

Step 2: Creating the Backlog

Once the product vision is in place, the **Product Owner** works with stakeholders to gather **user stories** and tasks that represent what the product needs. The backlog items (often referred to as **Product Backlog Items** or **PBIs**) should include everything from new features to bug fixes, technical debt, and other tasks that add value to the product.

- **Tip**: When creating the backlog, avoid the temptation to add too many items at once. Start with the **MVP** (Minimum Viable Product) and build from there, refining and adding items based on user feedback and market demands.

Step 3: Prioritizing the Backlog

Once the backlog is created, the next challenge is prioritizing the items. Not all tasks have equal value, and it's the Product Owner's responsibility to ensure that the most valuable tasks are worked on first. Prioritization should be based on factors such as:

- **Customer Value**: How important is this feature to the end user?

- **Business Impact**: Does this task contribute to key business goals like increasing revenue or user engagement?

- **Technical Feasibility**: Is the task realistic to complete given the current technical constraints?

- **Example**: In a startup developing a fitness app, the Product Owner might prioritize features like "personalized workout plans" higher than "dark mode" because the former adds more value to the customer experience, even though dark mode is a nice-to-have.

Best Practice Tip: Use a prioritization framework like **MoSCoW** (Must-have, Should-have, Could-have, Won't-have) to categorize backlog items. This helps the team focus on high-priority tasks and avoid wasting time on low-value features.

Writing Effective User Stories

At the core of every **Product Backlog** are **user stories**—concise, clear descriptions of a feature or task from the perspective of the end user. User stories help the development team understand what needs to be built and why. Well-written user stories form the foundation for successful Sprint Planning and execution.

Structure of a User Story

A typical user story follows this structure:

- **As a [user role], I want [desired feature] so that [reason or benefit].**

This format ensures that the story focuses on the user's needs, not just the technical requirements. Writing user stories in this way helps the team stay customer-centric and prioritize tasks that deliver real value.

- **Example**: "As a user, I want to be able to schedule virtual workout sessions with trainers so that I can plan my fitness routine in advance."

Applying the INVEST Criteria

The **INVEST** acronym is a helpful guideline for writing high-quality user stories. Each user story should be:

- Independent: The story should be self-contained, with no overlap or dependencies on other stories. This allows the team to prioritize and develop the story without waiting for other tasks to be completed.

  - **Example**: A user story for implementing notifications should not depend on another story for designing the user interface. Each task can be developed independently.

- Negotiable: The story is not a rigid contract but an invitation for discussion. The **Product Owner** and **Development Team** should collaborate on the best way to achieve the desired outcome.

  - **Tip**: Encourage conversations about the user story during Sprint Planning or backlog refinement sessions to explore different approaches.

- **V**aluable: Each story must deliver value to the customer or the business. This ensures the team focuses on tasks that matter.

    - **Example**: A story that allows users to save their favorite workouts would be valuable because it improves user engagement and retention, directly contributing to business goals.

- **E**stimable: The story must be clear enough that the team can estimate the effort required to complete it. If the team can't estimate the story, it may be too vague or too large.

    - **Tip**: If a user story is too complex or unclear, break it down into smaller stories until each one can be estimated.

- **S**mall: A good user story should be small enough to be completed within a single sprint. Large stories, or **epics**, should be broken down into more manageable pieces.

    - **Example**: Instead of a broad story like "Build the entire payment system," break it down into smaller stories, such as "Implement credit card payment" and "Set up PayPal integration."

- **T**estable: Each story should have clear **acceptance criteria** that define what "done" means. These criteria allow the team to test whether the story has been successfully completed.

    - **Example**: For a story that involves sending email notifications, the acceptance criteria might include: "An email is sent when a new workout is scheduled,"

> and "The email includes the correct workout details and time."
>
> By following the **INVEST** model, teams can ensure that each user story is well-defined, actionable and valuable. This reduces ambiguity and increases the chances of delivering the right product to customers.

Writing Acceptance Criteria

In addition to the user story, each backlog item should include **acceptance criteria**—the conditions that must be met for the task to be considered complete. Acceptance criteria help ensure that the team understands what "done" looks like and reduces the chances of miscommunication between the Product Owner and the development team.

- **Example**: For the user story about scheduling virtual workouts, the acceptance criteria might be:

  1. Users can view available time slots for trainers.

  2. Users can select a time slot and confirm their booking.

  3. Users receive an email confirmation after scheduling a session.

Best Practice Tip: Keep acceptance criteria as clear and concise as possible. Use bullet points to break down the requirements and ensure that they can be easily tested.

Managing and Refining the Backlog

The **Product Backlog** is not a static document. It evolves as the product grows, as new ideas emerge, and as feedback is received. **Backlog refinement** (or **grooming**) is an ongoing process where the Product Owner and the development team regularly review, update, and refine the backlog to ensure it reflects the current priorities and goals.

Regular Backlog Refinement

Backlog refinement should occur on a regular basis, ideally every sprint. During these refinement sessions, the team reviews the items at the top of the backlog and ensures they are well defined and ready to be worked on in the next sprint.

- **Tip**: Don't wait until Sprint Planning to refine backlog items. Refinement should be an ongoing process, so that when Sprint Planning occurs, the team can quickly pull ready-to-go tasks from the top of the backlog.

Prioritization Based on Feedback

As new information becomes available—whether from user feedback, market changes, or technical discoveries—the Product Owner should revisit the backlog to adjust priorities. Features that seemed important a month ago may no longer be relevant, while new opportunities may arise that demand immediate attention.

- **Example**: A social media startup might initially prioritize building a content recommendation engine. However, after receiving feedback that users are struggling with account creation, the team might decide to prioritize improving the sign-up process over the recommendation feature.

Managing Technical Debt

In addition to user stories, the Product Backlog should also include **technical debt**—those parts of the codebase that require cleanup or refactoring but do not directly impact the end user. Managing technical debt is critical to ensuring that the product remains scalable and maintainable.

- **Best Practice**: Regularly allocate time in each sprint for the development team to address technical debt. If left unchecked, technical debt can accumulate and slow down future development.

Planning Poker: A Collaborative Estimation Technique

Planning Poker is a widely used Agile estimation technique that helps Scrum teams collaboratively estimate the effort required to complete backlog items, such as user stories. It encourages participation from all team members, leading to more accurate and consensus-driven estimates.

In a typical **Planning Poker session**, each team member is given a set of cards with numbers representing the relative size or effort (often following the **Fibonacci sequence**: 1, 2, 3, 5, 8, 13, etc.). The Product Owner presents a user story, and the team discusses it briefly. After the discussion, each team member selects a card privately, representing their estimate of how much effort the task will take. Once everyone has made their selection, the cards are revealed simultaneously.

If there's a significant difference in the estimates, the team discusses the reasons behind the variations. Team members with the highest and lowest estimates explain their reasoning, and the discussion continues until the group reaches a consensus. The process helps uncover assumptions, clarify uncertainties, and ensure that the entire team shares an understanding of the work involved.

Why It's Effective: Planning Poker is valuable because it encourages engagement from the whole team and avoids the biases that can occur when estimates are given verbally. It also promotes deeper discussions about each task, which leads to more accurate estimates and stronger team alignment.

Case Study: A Product Owner Working with Stakeholders to Prioritize Features

Let's look at an example of a **startup called FoodNow**, which is building a food delivery app. The Product Owner, Emily, is responsible for managing the backlog and prioritizing features. The company's stakeholders include marketing teams, customer support, and key investors.

Step 1: Gathering Stakeholder Input

During a stakeholder meeting, the marketing team emphasizes the need for a feature that allows users to order from multiple restaurants in a single delivery. Meanwhile, the customer support team highlights ongoing issues with the payment system, and the investors are focused on increasing user engagement through personalized recommendations.

Emily listens to each team's input and adds their requests to the Product Backlog.

Step 2: Prioritizing Features

Using the **MoSCoW** prioritization framework, Emily categorizes the tasks as follows:

- **Must have**: Fix payment system issues (based on customer support feedback)

- **Should have**: Add personalized recommendations to improve engagement (based on investor feedback)

- **Could have**: Allow users to order from multiple restaurants (marketing team request)

In this case, fixing the payment system is the top priority because it directly affects the user experience and revenue. Personalized recommendations are also important but not as urgent, while the multiple-restaurant feature is a nice-to-have that can be addressed later.

Step 3: Refining and Assigning User Stories

Emily refines each backlog item, ensuring it has well-defined user stories and acceptance criteria. For the payment system, she writes the following user story:

- **As a user, I want to securely save my payment details so that I can quickly complete my order without re-entering my information.**

She also includes acceptance criteria, such as:

- Users can securely store credit card information.

- Users receive a confirmation message after payment details are saved.

- Payment details are encrypted to ensure security.

Step 4: Continuous Refinement and Feedback

Throughout the development process, Emily continues to gather feedback from stakeholders and users, refining the backlog accordingly. After the payment issue is resolved, she shifts focus to the personalized recommendation feature, ensuring that the backlog remains dynamic and responsive to changing needs.

Key Takeaways

- The Product Backlog is the heart of Scrum's planning process, serving as the single source of truth for the tasks and features needed to build the product.

- A clear and well-defined product vision is essential before creating the backlog to ensure alignment and direction throughout the development process.

- Prioritizing the backlog based on customer value, business impact, and technical feasibility ensures that the team is always working on the most important tasks.

- Writing effective user stories that follow the INVEST criteria (Independent, Negotiable, Valuable, Estimable, Small, and Testable) improves clarity and ensures stories are actionable.

- Acceptance criteria for user stories provide clear definitions of what "done" means and reduce the chances of miscommunication between the Product Owner and the development team.

- Regular backlog refinement sessions help keep the backlog up to date, ensuring that tasks are ready for upcoming sprints and aligned with evolving priorities.

- Managing technical debt is as important as delivering features, as it ensures that the product remains scalable and maintainable over time.

- Planning Poker is a collaborative estimation technique that promotes deeper discussions about backlog items, leading to more accurate estimates and better team alignment.

- Continuous feedback from stakeholders and users helps refine the backlog and adjust priorities, ensuring that the product stays relevant and meets user needs.

- A well-managed backlog helps teams focus on the most valuable tasks, contributing directly to business growth and customer satisfaction.

Chapter 5

Scaling Scrum in a Growing Startup

*"The most efficient and effective method of
conveying information to and within a development
team is face-to-face conversation."*

As startups grow, the need to scale Scrum to accommodate more teams and complex workflows becomes inevitable. Scrum, which works well for small, autonomous teams, needs adjustments when scaling across multiple teams working on different aspects of a product. The key is maintaining the agility, collaboration, and customer focus that made Scrum successful in the early stages. This chapter explores how to adapt Scrum for larger teams, coordinate multiple Scrum teams, and leverage frameworks like **Scrum of Scrums**, **SAFe**, **LeSS**, **Nexus**, **DAD**, and **Scrum@Scale** to scale effectively. We'll also include a case study of a startup expanding its teams using Scrum of Scrums framework.

Adapting Scrum for Larger Teams

In small startups, Scrum works well with a single team of fewer than ten people. As the company grows, scaling becomes challenging, requiring adjustments to maintain agility without introducing bureaucracy.

Challenges of Scaling Scrum

1. **Coordination Across Teams**: With multiple Scrum teams, there's a risk of misalignment if the work and goals are not well-coordinated.

2. **Maintaining Agile Culture**: As organizations grow, processes often become more formal, threatening to dilute the agile mindset.

3. **Increased Communication Needs**: Larger teams mean more communication is needed to ensure everyone stays aligned, which can lead to delays and bottlenecks.

Solutions: Keeping Scrum Agile While Scaling

1. **Smaller Cross-Functional Teams**: Instead of growing a single team, break them into smaller, independent Scrum teams, each responsible for different product features or components. This keeps decision-making fast and agile.

2. **Clear Vision and Alignment**: Ensure that all teams are aligned with a clear product vision and overarching goals. This helps prevent duplication of work and keeps all teams on the same page.

3. **Leadership Empowerment**: Leaders must guide teams without micromanaging them. Empowered teams with clear objectives are more efficient and better equipped to scale.

Coordinating Multiple Scrum Teams

As the number of teams increases, **cross-team coordination** becomes vital. Maintaining agility while preventing communication silos is a delicate balancing act. Frameworks like **Scrum of Scrums**, **SAFe**, and **LeSS** help coordinate multiple Scrum teams effectively.

Scrum of Scrums

Scrum of Scrums is a coordination method for scaling Scrum. It works by having representatives from each team meet regularly to align on goals, resolve dependencies, and discuss progress.

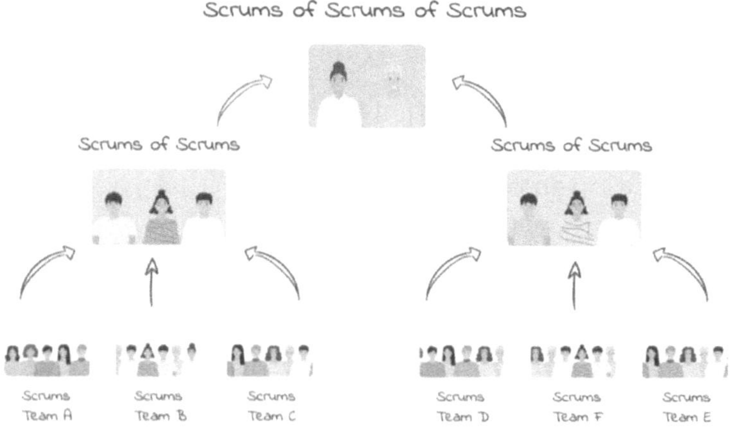

Source: https://hygger.io/guides/agile/scrum/scrum-of-scrums/

How Scrum of Scrums Works:

1. **Team Representatives**: Each Scrum team appoints a representative to attend the Scrum of Scrums meeting. These representatives discuss progress, dependencies, and challenges that need to be addressed.

2. **Regular Meetings**: Scrum of Scrums meetings are held weekly or bi-weekly, providing a regular cadence for cross-team coordination.

3. **Autonomy with Alignment**: The framework allows teams to remain autonomous while ensuring they are aligned with the larger product vision and goals.

Scrum of Scrums is lightweight and works well for startups that are growing but want to avoid heavy processes.

Scaling Frameworks: SAFe, LeSS, Nexus and More

While **Scrum of Scrums** is great for small-to-mid-sized organizations, as companies scale further, more structured frameworks like **SAFe**, **LeSS**, **Nexus**, and **Disciplined Agile Delivery (DAD)** offer greater flexibility for larger teams and portfolios.

SAFe (Scaled Agile Framework)

SAFe is a widely adopted framework that organizes agile teams at different levels—team, program, and portfolio. It provides a structure for scaling Agile practices across an entire enterprise.

Key Features of SAFe:

1. **Agile Release Trains (ARTs)**: In SAFe, multiple Scrum teams are organized into Agile Release Trains, groups of teams working together towards a common product goal.

2. **PI Planning (Program Increment Planning)**: SAFe introduces PI Planning, which is a longer-term planning event

(typically 8-12 weeks) that helps synchronize the teams' work and ensures alignment with business objectives.

3. **Roles and Responsibilities**: SAFe adds roles such as **Release Train Engineers**, **Solution Managers**, and **Epic Owners** to manage the complexities of scaling across multiple teams and portfolios.

SAFe is suitable for large organizations with complex projects that require coordination between many teams working on interdependent tasks.

LeSS (Large-Scale Scrum)

LeSS offers a simpler approach to scaling Scrum by maintaining one Product Backlog, one Product Owner, and one unified sprint across multiple teams. It avoids the layers of roles and processes introduced in other frameworks.

Key Features of LeSS:

1. **One Product Backlog**: All teams work from the same Product Backlog, ensuring consistency in priorities and goals.

2. **One Product Owner**: There's a single Product Owner responsible for managing the backlog and ensuring that teams work on the most valuable features.

3. **Coordination and Integration**: Teams coordinate closely to ensure that all work integrates smoothly, minimizing cross-team dependencies.

LeSS is ideal for organizations that want to scale Scrum without introducing much complexity, especially when the product development involves up to eight teams.

Nexus

Nexus is another Scrum-based framework designed for organizations that need to scale Scrum across multiple teams. It focuses on reducing the complexity of scaling by introducing a **Nexus Integration Team** that ensures the work from multiple teams integrates smoothly.

Key Features of Nexus:

1. **Nexus Integration Team**: This team is responsible for managing the dependencies and integration challenges that arise when multiple teams work on the same product.

2. **Cross-Team Refinement**: Nexus requires cross-team backlog refinement sessions to ensure that technical dependencies are identified early and managed effectively.

3. **Sprint Events**: Nexus builds on the existing Scrum events, with a focus on integrating the work from multiple teams into a single product increment.

Nexus is ideal for startups working on complex products where multiple teams need to integrate their work frequently.

Disciplined Agile Delivery (DAD)

Disciplined Agile Delivery (DAD) goes beyond Scrum by incorporating the full delivery lifecycle, including inception, construction, transition, and deployment. DAD is designed for organizations that need to scale Scrum to include non-development activities, such as **DevOps** and **security**.

Key Features of DAD:

1. **Full Lifecycle Coverage**: Unlike Scrum, which focuses primarily on development, DAD covers the entire delivery lifecycle, from product conception to release.

2. **DevOps Integration**: DAD integrates DevOps practices into the Agile framework, emphasizing continuous delivery and operations.

3. **Methodology Choice**: DAD allows teams to choose the best Agile method for their context, whether it's Scrum, Kanban, or Lean.

DAD is suitable for organizations that need to integrate agile practices across development, operations, and other business functions.

Scrum@Scale

Scrum@Scale is a lightweight framework that uses two interlinked cycles—the **Scrum Master Cycle** and the **Product Owner Cycle**—to scale Scrum across large organizations. It focuses on aligning product development with the company's strategic vision.

Key Features of Scrum@Scale:

1. **Scrum Master and Product Owner Cycles**: These two cycles ensure that product development is aligned with the company's strategic goals, while maintaining agility at the team level.

2. **Scrum of Scrums Master**: This role facilitates cross-team coordination, ensuring that dependencies and risks are managed across teams.

Scrum@Scale is ideal for startups that want to scale without adding significant complexity to their processes.

Scaling Frameworks: A Comparison

For startups that continue to grow rapidly, scaling beyond Scrum of Scrum may require more structured frameworks. **SAFe**, **LeSS**, **Nexus**, **Disciplined Agile Delivery (DAD)**, and **Scrum@Scale** provide different approaches to scaling Scrum based on the organization's size, project complexity, and need for coordination.

Framework	Best for	Key Features	Complexity
Scrum of Scrums	Small to mid-sized teams	Cross-team coordination via representatives	Low
Nexus	Mid to large teams working on a single product	Nexus Integration Team for managing dependencies	Moderate
LeSS	Large organizations with up to 8 teams per product area	One Product Owner, one Backlog	Moderate

Frame-work	Best for	Key Features	Complex-ity
SAFe	Large enterprises with complex projects	Agile Release Trains, PI Planning	High
DAD	Organizations with complex DevOps and security needs	Full lifecycle coverage from inception to deployment	High
Scrum@ Scale	Growing organizations seeking to scale with minimal complexity	Scrum Master and Product Owner Cycles	Low

Case Study: A Startup Expanding and Implementing Scrum of Scrums

Let's take the example of **TechFlow**, a startup building AI-powered analytics tools. Initially, TechFlow operated with one Scrum team. However, as the company expanded to five Scrum teams working on different aspects of the product, managing communication and coordination became increasingly complex. To maintain agility and alignment, they implemented **Scrum of Scrums**.

Step 1: Defining Teams and Responsibilities

TechFlow's product team expanded into five Scrum teams, each responsible for a different aspect of the product:

- **Data Integration Team**: Responsible for integrating external datasets into the platform.

- **UI Team**: Focused on designing and implementing the user interface.

- **Machine Learning Team**: Developing AI models for predictive analytics.

- **API Team**: Building the backend API for external integrations.

- **Customer Support Team**: Ensuring a smooth onboarding process for customers integrating with the platform.

Step 2: Implementing Scrum of Scrums

To ensure smooth coordination between the teams, TechFlow introduced **Scrum of Scrums**:

- Each team appointed a representative (usually the Scrum Master) to participate in a weekly Scrum of Scrums meeting.

- The meeting focused on discussing cross-team dependencies, sharing progress updates, and identifying roadblocks that might impact other teams. For example, the API team needed timely data from the Data Integration Team for their work to progress.

- The representatives worked together to resolve issues and ensure that all teams remained aligned on the overall product goals.

Results

By implementing Scrum of Scrums, TechFlow achieved the following:

- **Improved Coordination**: The weekly meetings allowed teams to stay aligned, reducing communication bottlenecks and preventing overlapping work.

- **Faster Problem-Solving**: Cross-team dependencies were identified and addressed early, minimizing delays caused by integration issues.

- **Maintained Agility**: Despite expanding into five teams, TechFlow maintained the agility and speed that had fueled its initial success.

Key Takeaways

- Scaling Scrum becomes essential as startups grow, requiring adjustments to maintain agility across multiple teams and complex workflows.

- Challenges of scaling include coordination across teams, maintaining an Agile culture, and handling increased communication needs.

- Smaller cross-functional teams help preserve agility by breaking large teams into smaller, autonomous Scrum teams responsible for specific product components.

- Scrum of Scrums is an effective coordination framework for scaling Scrum in startups, ensuring alignment and communication across multiple teams through regular representative meetings.

- Frameworks like SAFe (Scaled Agile Framework), LeSS (Large-Scale Scrum), and Nexus provide structured approaches for scaling Scrum in larger organizations with complex product portfolios.

- SAFe introduces key elements such as Agile Release Trains (ARTs) and Program Increment (PI) Planning to synchronize work across many Scrum teams in larger enterprises.

- LeSS simplifies scaling by maintaining a single Product Backlog and a unified sprint across teams, making it ideal for organizations with fewer layers of roles.

- Nexus adds a Nexus Integration Team to manage dependencies and integration across Scrum teams working on a shared product.

- Disciplined Agile Delivery (DAD) incorporates non-development activities, such as DevOps and security, for organizations needing to scale Agile beyond development teams.

- A tailored framework, whether Scrum of Scrums, SAFe, or Nexus, allows startups to scale effectively while maintaining the flexibility and collaboration that originally made Scrum successful.

Chapter 6

Enhancing Team Collaboration and Communication

❖

*"Working software is the primary
measure of progress."*

Team collaboration and communication are at the heart of an effective Scrum team. As startups grow, especially in fast-paced environments, it becomes essential to foster a collaborative culture where team members work together efficiently and communicate effectively. This chapter covers strategies for building a collaborative team culture, enhancing communication, and utilizing tools and techniques for remote teams, all while aligning with the key Scrum ceremonies. Additionally, we'll highlight the importance of stakeholder collaboration.

Building a Collaborative Team Culture

A collaborative team culture is crucial for a startup's success, as it ensures that team members work cohesively toward shared goals. Fostering such a culture is foundational to effective Scrum practices and ensures that each ceremony – Sprint Planning, Daily Stand-ups, Reviews, and Retrospectives – leads to productive outcomes.

Key Strategies for Fostering Collaboration

1. **Shared Vision and Goals**: To collaborate effectively, team members must be aligned with the startup's vision and goals. Regularly communicate the vision and how each team member's work contributes to the bigger picture. In Scrum, this is reinforced during **Sprint Planning**, where the team sets the sprint goals that align with the product vision.

   - **Example**: During Sprint Planning, emphasize how the sprint goal ties into the larger product roadmap, ensuring everyone understands their role in achieving it.

2. **Trust and Respect**: Collaboration thrives when team members trust and respect one another. Open communication, active listening, and transparency build trust over time. Trust also plays a critical role in **Retrospectives**, where teams review their performance and share honest feedback.

   - **Tip**: During Retrospectives, ensure that feedback is constructive and everyone feels safe to speak up about what didn't work.

3. **Empowerment and Autonomy**: Empower teams to make decisions within their domain. Scrum encourages autonomy, especially during **Daily Stand-ups** and **Sprint Planning**, where team members decide how to achieve their goals.

   - **Example**: Allow teams to decide how they approach tasks during Sprint Planning, fostering ownership and responsibility.

4. **Clear Roles and Responsibilities**: Clarifying roles helps avoid confusion. In Scrum, the roles of the **Product Owner**, **Scrum**

Master, and **Development Team** must be clearly defined to ensure smooth collaboration.

- **Example**: During Sprint Planning, the Product Owner ensures the backlog is prioritized, while the Development Team determines how much work can be accomplished during the sprint.

5. **Recognition and Appreciation**: Recognizing contributions boosts morale. Celebrate successes in **Sprint Reviews**, where the team demonstrates the product increment and receives stakeholder feedback.

- **Tip**: Use Sprint Reviews as an opportunity to highlight team achievements and reinforce positive collaboration.

6. **Diverse and Inclusive Environment**: Teams perform better when diverse perspectives are valued. Diverse teams bring different ideas, enriching the **Sprint Retrospective** and helping solve problems creatively.

- **Tip**: Encourage diverse opinions during Retrospectives to explore innovative solutions.

7. **Team Building Activities**: Organizing team-building activities strengthens bonds. In Scrum, informal team-building can happen during **Retrospectives** or outside formal Scrum ceremonies to foster collaboration.

- **Tip**: Consider virtual team-building games or social activities that encourage camaraderie in distributed teams.

Effective Communication Strategies

Effective communication is the backbone of any successful Scrum team. Transparent and clear communication ensures alignment, accountability and continuous improvement. Scrum ceremonies offer built-in opportunities to enhance communication across the team.

Key Communication Practices

1. **Clear and Concise Communication**: In Scrum, teams must communicate clearly during all ceremonies. Whether it's Sprint Planning, Daily Stand-ups, or Reviews, clear communication ensures that the right priorities are set and addressed.

    *   **Tip**: Use simple, direct language in Daily Stand-ups and Sprint Reviews to prevent misunderstandings and ensure all stakeholders are aligned.

2. **Regular Check-ins**: **Daily Stand-ups** provide an ideal opportunity for regular check-ins. These 15-minute sessions keep the team aligned, ensure that work is progressing smoothly, and allow for quick identification of blockers.

    *   **Example**: During a Daily Stand-up, team members share what they accomplished yesterday, what they'll work on today, and any challenges they're facing.

3. **Active Listening**: Encourage active listening, especially during **Retrospectives** and **Sprint Reviews**. Listening ensures that everyone feels heard and that feedback is acted upon.

    *   **Tip**: In Retrospectives, repeat back what's been said to ensure understanding and show that you're actively listening.

4. **Transparent Communication Channels**: Use transparent communication platforms where information is easily accessible. In Scrum, tools like Jira or Trello provide transparency into the team's progress by visually tracking tasks from Sprint Planning to completion.

   • **Tip**: Ensure that all project updates are documented in a shared location, accessible to both the team and stakeholders.

5. **Feedback Loops**: Scrum emphasizes continuous improvement through feedback loops. **Sprint Reviews** gather feedback from stakeholders, while **Retrospectives** focus on internal feedback to improve team processes.

   • **Tip**: In Retrospectives, identify specific actions for improvement and follow up during the next Retrospective to track progress.

6. **Conflict Resolution**: Conflicts are inevitable, but addressing them promptly is crucial for maintaining team harmony. In Scrum, **Retrospectives** are a safe space to discuss any conflicts that arose during the sprint.

   • **Example**: If a conflict arises over task ownership, use the Retrospective to discuss what went wrong and how to prevent it in the future.

Tools and Techniques for Remote Teams

In today's world, many startups operate with distributed or fully remote teams. Maintaining strong collaboration and communication in such environments requires the right tools and techniques, especially when participating in Scrum ceremonies remotely.

Tools for Remote Scrum Teams

1. **Video Conferencing**: Use tools like **Zoom**, **Microsoft Teams**, or **Google Meet** for virtual Sprint Planning, Daily Stand-ups, and Sprint Reviews. Face-to-face communication helps maintain engagement and trust.

   - **Example**: A remote team uses Zoom for their Sprint Planning meetings, ensuring that everyone can discuss backlog priorities and sprint goals in real-time.

2. **Collaboration Platforms**: Tools like **Slack** or **Microsoft Teams** enable real-time communication. Dedicated channels can be created for each project or sprint, keeping conversations organized.

   - **Tip**: Create dedicated Slack channels for different projects to avoid confusion and ensure that all discussions are centralized and accessible.

3. **Document Sharing and Project Management**: Use tools like **Google Drive** for document sharing and **Jira** or **Trello** for managing sprint tasks. These tools keep the entire team informed and up-to-date on project progress.

   - **Example**: In Sprint Planning, the Product Owner can use Jira to present the backlog, and the team can estimate and assign tasks directly within the tool.

4. **Time Zone Management**: When working across time zones, use tools like **World Time Buddy** to schedule Scrum ceremonies at convenient times for everyone.

   - **Tip**: Rotate meeting times to ensure that no team member is consistently disadvantaged by the time zone difference.

5. **Asynchronous Communication**: Encourage asynchronous communication for tasks that don't require immediate responses. Tools like Slack or email allow team members to respond when convenient.

   - **Example**: A remote team uses asynchronous updates for non-urgent Sprint Planning discussions, allowing team members in different time zones to contribute when they're available.

The Chicken and Pig Story: Commitment vs. Involvement in Scrum

Source:https://helpingimprove.com/agile-commitment-scrum-pig-chicken-part-1/

In Scrum, the tale of the **Chicken and the Pig** is often used to illustrate the difference between **commitment** and **involvement** within a team. Here's how the story goes: A chicken and a pig are having a conversation. The chicken suggests they open a restaurant. The pig is not so sure and asks what they would call it. The chicken replies **"Ham and**

Eggs?". The pig thinks for a moment and replies, "No thanks, you'd only be involved, but I'd be *committed*!"

This humorous story draws a clear line between being fully committed to a project and being merely involved. In Scrum, this analogy is used to explain the roles in a team. The **Scrum team**—consisting of the **Product Owner**, **Scrum Master**, and **Development Team**—are like the pig in the story: fully committed to delivering the Sprint goals. They are responsible for planning, building, and delivering the product, and their success depends on their shared commitment to meeting these objectives.

On the other hand, **stakeholders** and other external parties, like the chicken, are involved but not committed in the same way. They don't contribute directly to the work being done, but their feedback is essential for the team's progress. Stakeholders such as executives, clients, and end-users provide valuable input and guidance during **Sprint Reviews** and other touchpoints. Their involvement helps ensure that the product is on track and aligned with business goals, but they are not responsible for the day-to-day effort of delivery.

While the story humorously highlights the difference between commitment and involvement, both roles are critical to the success of a Scrum team. The team needs to be fully committed to the sprint goals but also rely on stakeholders' involvement to gather feedback and ensure that the product delivers value to the business.

Case Study: A Remote Startup Using Video Calls and Collaboration Tools for Daily Stand-ups

Startup: TechRemote, a SaaS startup developing project management tools, operates remotely with team members in the U.S., Europe, and Asia. The team faced challenges in maintaining daily alignment across time zones and keeping collaboration fluid.

Step 1: Implementing Daily Stand-ups via Zoom

TechRemote introduced 15-minute Daily Stand-ups using Zoom, scheduled to accommodate all time zones. Team members share their progress, plans for the day, and any blockers, ensuring continuous alignment.

Step 2: Using Slack for Asynchronous Communication

TechRemote uses **Slack** to maintain communication across time zones. With dedicated channels for different projects, team members can post updates, ask questions, and respond asynchronously.

Step 3: Project Tracking via Jira

The team uses **Jira** for task tracking and Sprint Planning. All tasks are visible to the entire team, and progress is updated in real time, ensuring that everyone is aligned and informed about the current work.

Outcome:

By integrating video conferencing for Daily Stand-ups, Slack for asynchronous updates, and Jira for sprint tracking, TechRemote improved its communication and collaboration, leading to increased productivity and more efficient sprint cycles.

Key Takeaways

- Building a collaborative team culture is essential for startups, ensuring that team members align with shared goals and work cohesively toward success.

- Regularly communicating the startup's vision during Scrum ceremonies helps keep team members engaged and focused on achieving sprint goals.

- Trust and respect are foundational to successful collaboration. Open communication, active listening, and transparency foster trust within the team, especially during Retrospectives.

- Empowering teams to make decisions during Sprint Planning and Daily Stand-ups promotes autonomy, ownership, and accountability in achieving sprint objectives.

- Clear roles and responsibilities in Scrum, such as those of the Product Owner, Scrum Master, and Development Team, help avoid confusion and improve coordination.

- Effective communication strategies ensure alignment and continuous improvement. Regular check-ins, active listening, and transparent communication channels like Jira and Trello improve team dynamics.

- Remote teams require special attention to communication, and tools like Zoom, Slack, and Jira help distributed teams collaborate effectively and stay aligned.

- Utilizing feedback loops through Sprint Reviews and Retrospectives ensures continuous improvement and helps teams adapt to challenges quickly.

- Asynchronous communication through tools like Slack can improve collaboration for teams working across different time zones, allowing flexibility in task management.

- Stakeholder involvement is crucial for feedback, but commitment from the core Scrum team is key to successfully delivering on sprint goals.

Chapter 7

Measuring Success and Continuous Improvement

*"Agile processes promote sustainable development.
The sponsors, developers and users should be able to
maintain a constant pace indefinitely."*

In the dynamic world of startups, measuring success and fostering continuous improvement are essential for sustaining growth and innovation. Scrum, by its very nature, promotes regular reflection on performance and iterative improvements. This chapter explores the key performance indicators (KPIs) used by Scrum teams, the importance of metrics in driving improvement, and the role of Retrospectives in continuous learning.

Key Performance Indicators (KPIs) for Scrum Teams

KPIs are a vital part of assessing team performance and making data-driven decisions. By tracking these indicators, teams can visualize progress, pinpoint inefficiencies, and ensure alignment with the overall product vision.

Definition and Importance of KPIs

Key Performance Indicators (KPIs) are measurable values that demonstrate how effectively a team is achieving its key business objectives. For Scrum teams, KPIs provide crucial insights into the team's productivity, quality, and ability to deliver on sprint goals. These metrics help identify both successes and areas needing improvement, offering a solid foundation for data-driven decision-making.

- **Example**: A startup working on a mobile application tracks its velocity to determine how much work its team can complete in each sprint. By understanding its capacity, the team can better forecast future sprints and make more realistic commitments.

Common KPIs in Scrum

1. **Velocity**: This measures the amount of work (in story points or hours) that a team completes in a sprint. It is a key indicator of a team's capacity and is often used for Sprint Planning.

   - **Example**: A Scrum team completes an average of 40 story points per sprint. This helps the Product Owner forecast the timeline for future features and prioritize the backlog accordingly.

2. **Sprint Burndown**: This chart visualizes the remaining work in a sprint. It helps track whether the team is on target to complete all sprint tasks by the end of the sprint.

   - **Example**: If the burndown chart shows that too many tasks remain toward the end of the sprint, the team can assess whether the scope needs to be adjusted or additional resources allocated.

3. **Cycle Time**: This measures the time it takes to complete a task from start to finish. Teams use it to identify inefficiencies in their process and streamline workflows.

    - **Example**: If the cycle time for user story implementation is increasing, the team can investigate bottlenecks such as resource allocation or technical challenges.

4. **Defect Density**: This tracks the number of defects per unit of work. It helps maintain product quality by identifying areas that need attention.

    - **Tip**: By reviewing the defect density of each sprint, teams can focus on improving code quality and refining their testing process.

5. **Customer Satisfaction**: This metric evaluates how satisfied customers are with the product or service. It can be measured through surveys, Net Promoter Score (NPS), or customer feedback.

    - **Example**: After every product release, a startup surveys its customers, asking for feedback on new features, usability, and overall satisfaction. The insights help prioritize future backlog items.

Selecting the Right KPIs

The choice of KPIs depends on the startup's goals and challenges. It's essential to pick KPIs that align with both the product vision and business objectives while also being actionable. Review and adjust KPIs regularly to ensure they remain relevant as your startup evolves.

- **Tip**: If your team is struggling with meeting sprint commitments, prioritize tracking velocity and sprint burndown. For teams focused on improving product quality, defect density and customer satisfaction would be more relevant KPIs.

Using Metrics to Drive Improvement

The power of KPIs lies in how teams use them to foster improvement. Collecting data is only the first step; the real value comes from analyzing metrics, identifying trends, and making informed decisions that drive team performance and product quality.

Collecting and Analyzing Data

Start by tracking metrics through tools like **Jira**, **Trello**, or **Azure DevOps**. These platforms automate data collection and provide teams with insights into their progress. Gather data on velocity, cycle time, defect density, and other metrics that reflect your team's performance.

Once data is collected, the next step is analysis. Look for patterns and correlations between different metrics to identify the root cause of any issues. For instance, if a team's velocity is inconsistent across sprints, further analysis may reveal issues with task estimation or unexpected technical challenges.

Identifying Trends and Patterns

Regularly reviewing metrics allows teams to uncover trends that impact performance. Identifying these patterns early helps teams take corrective action before problems escalate.

- **Example**: If you notice that defect density spikes after every feature release, it might indicate that your team is rushing through testing in the final sprint stages. This pattern suggests the need for more thorough testing earlier in the sprint cycle.

Making Data-Driven Decisions

Once the data has been analyzed, it's time to implement changes that improve team performance. Use the insights gained to refine Sprint Planning, resource allocation, and workflows. For instance, if metrics indicate that cycle time is increasing due to bottlenecks in development, the team can experiment with alternative workflows to reduce waiting times and improve task completion rates.

- **Tip**: Don't just track KPIs for the sake of tracking. Ensure that every metric you follow leads to actionable insights that can be tested and measured again for improvement.

Best Practices for Using Metrics

1. **Establish Baselines**: Establish baseline metrics to track improvements over time. For instance, knowing your team's average velocity allows you to measure progress across future sprints.

2. **Involve the Team**: Engage the entire Scrum team in collecting and analyzing data to foster ownership and collaboration.

3. **Review Metrics Regularly**: Conduct regular reviews of metrics at the end of each sprint to assess progress and adjust the backlog or sprint goals accordingly.

4. **Balance Quantitative and Qualitative Data**: Use both quantitative metrics like velocity and qualitative feedback from Retrospectives and customer feedback to get a complete view of performance.

Conducting Effective Retrospectives

Retrospectives are a core component of Scrum, providing the team with an opportunity to reflect on their performance and discuss ways to improve. The retrospective is where data-driven insights are transformed into actionable improvements.

Purpose and Benefits of Retrospectives

The goal of the retrospective is to foster a culture of **continuous improvement**. By looking back at the sprint, the team can identify what worked well, what didn't, and how to improve going forward. It promotes transparency and encourages the team to take responsibility for its successes and failures.

- **Tip**: Use Retrospectives to reinforce the importance of data-driven decision-making. Review velocity charts, sprint burndown charts, and cycle time data to guide the conversation.

Techniques for Conducting Retrospectives

Several retrospective techniques can be used to keep sessions engaging and productive:

1. **Start, Stop, Continue**: This technique asks the team to reflect on what they should start doing, stop doing, and continue doing. It's simple and effective for identifying actionable improvements.

2. **4Ls (Liked, Learned, Lacked, Longed For)**: This method encourages team members to share what they liked about the sprint, what they learned, what they lacked, and what they longed for. It captures a wide range of feedback from both a technical and emotional perspective.

3. **Mad, Sad, Glad**: This technique allows team members to express their emotions about the sprint. It's particularly useful for addressing emotional issues that may be affecting team morale.

Implementing Changes Based on Retrospective Insights

Retrospective insights are only valuable if they lead to action. After identifying areas for improvement, assign ownership to team members for implementing changes and track the impact of those changes in the following sprint.

*   **Tip**: Follow up on action items from Retrospectives in the next sprint to ensure that improvements are being implemented and monitored.

Earned Value Management in Scrum: A New Perspective

Earned Value Management (EVM) is a core principle in traditional project management, especially in **Waterfall methodologies**. EVM measures project performance by analyzing scope, cost, and schedule, providing insights into budget utilization and progress against predefined milestones. In the Waterfall approach, where tasks are laid out in linear phases, EVM fits naturally, offering precise snapshots of project health at every stage.

However, applying EVM in an **Agile Scrum environment** poses unique challenges due to the inherent flexibility of Agile. Scrum's iterative, adaptive approach doesn't revolve around a fixed scope, making the traditional EVM metrics—such as Planned Value (PV), Earned Value (EV), and Actual

---

Cost (AC)—difficult to measure as rigidly as in a waterfall. Yet, this flexibility is Scrum's strength. Agile Scrum provides **dynamic alternatives** to track progress, quality, and budget while adapting to change:

- **Burndown and Burnup Charts** track progress on deliverables against sprint goals, offering immediate insight into velocity and completion rates.

- **Velocity tracking** enables capacity assessment and future Sprint Planning, allowing teams to forecast deliverables realistically.

- **Sprint Reviews** with stakeholders and **Retrospectives** provide continuous feedback loops, enabling teams to make incremental adjustments to scope and approach.

- **Definition of Done (DoD)** ensures that each increment meets quality standards, maintaining control over scope and quality as the project evolves.

Pros of EVM in Agile: EVM can still offer value in Agile when used to manage high-level budgets or timelines, especially in larger enterprises or when working with fixed-bid contracts. It provides high-level insights into the overall project health without compromising Agile's flexibility.

Cons of EVM in Agile: The rigidity of traditional EVM metrics can clash with Agile's adaptable nature, often creating unnecessary pressure to meet cost and scope measures at the expense of adaptability and team creativity.

By embracing Agile's methods for tracking **cost, schedule, and scope**, Scrum teams gain real-time visibility, empowering them to deliver quality products iteratively while meeting business objectives. Although EVM's traditional metrics might not directly align with Agile, Scrum's adaptive metrics offer **equally effective—and often more actionable—ways of ensuring project success.**

Case Study: InnoTech Using Velocity Charts and Burndown Charts to Track Progress

InnoTech, a startup developing project management software, faced challenges with inaccurate Sprint Planning and high defect density in the early stages of using Scrum. To address these issues, they adopted metrics like velocity and sprint burndown to track progress and drive continuous improvement.

KPIs Tracked by InnoTech

1. **Velocity**: InnoTech tracks the number of story points completed in each sprint. This helps the team understand its capacity and plan future sprints more accurately.

2. **Sprint Burndown**: The burndown chart helps monitor the remaining work and identify bottlenecks early.

3. **Cycle Time**: By tracking cycle time, InnoTech identified inefficiencies in its workflow, particularly in handoffs between development and testing.

4. **Defect Density**: InnoTech tracks defect density to maintain product quality, especially during major feature releases.

Continuous Improvement at InnoTech

By reviewing their velocity and burndown charts at the end of each sprint, the team was able to set more realistic goals and improve Sprint Planning accuracy. The team also used retrospective feedback to adjust workflows, improving overall efficiency and reducing defect density.

Key Takeaways

- Key Performance Indicators (KPIs) are vital for assessing Scrum team performance and driving data-driven decision-making to align with product goals.

- Common Scrum KPIs include velocity, sprint burndown, cycle time, defect density, and customer satisfaction, each offering insights into team productivity and product quality.

- Velocity measures the team's capacity to deliver work in a sprint, aiding in Sprint Planning and forecasting future workload.

- Sprint burndown charts help track progress within a sprint, identifying whether the team is on pace to complete all sprint goals on time.

- Cycle time measures the time it takes to complete a task from start to finish, highlighting bottlenecks and inefficiencies in workflows.

- Defect density tracks the quality of the product by measuring the number of defects relative to the work completed, allowing teams to address quality issues early.

- Regularly reviewing metrics helps teams identify patterns, adjust workflows, and improve Sprint Planning accuracy.

- Effective Retrospectives enable teams to reflect on sprint outcomes, review metrics, and implement changes for continuous improvement.

- Tools like Jira, Trello, and Azure DevOps automate data collection, allowing teams to easily track KPIs and analyze performance trends.

- Measuring success in Scrum involves balancing both quantitative metrics and qualitative feedback, ensuring teams continuously improve while maintaining product quality.

Chapter 8

Overcoming Common Challenges

"Continuous attention to technical excellence and good design enhances agility."

In any organization adopting Scrum, teams are bound to face challenges that can hinder their progress. From resistance to change to managing resources efficiently, navigating these issues is critical to maintaining the team's productivity and overall success. This chapter explores some of the most common challenges that Scrum teams face and offers practical solutions for overcoming them.

Addressing Resistance to Change

Resistance to change is one of the most common obstacles encountered when implementing Scrum, especially in teams that have grown accustomed to traditional project management methods, such as **Waterfall**. Teams may resist Scrum's iterative nature, the emphasis on transparency, or the constant feedback loops inherent in Scrum ceremonies. Addressing this resistance is key to ensuring the successful adoption of Scrum.

Common Causes of Resistance

1. **Fear of Uncertainty**: Team members accustomed to rigid planning may fear the uncertainty that comes with iterative development. The lack of a detailed long-term plan can make some people uncomfortable.

2. **Lack of Understanding**: Many teams may not fully understand how Scrum works or its benefits. This can create confusion and resistance, as team members might see it as just "more meetings" or additional overhead.

3. **Cultural Resistance**: Organizational culture plays a huge role in the adoption of Scrum. A culture that values hierarchical decision-making, for example, may resist the more collaborative and self-organizing nature of Scrum.

Solutions to Overcome Resistance

1. **Education and Training**: Offer thorough training on Scrum principles and how they benefit the team. Hold workshops, introduce **Scrum coaches**, and encourage team members to attend Scrum events like **Sprint Planning** or **Daily Stand-ups** to see how the process works in action.

    *   **Example**: A product development team was hesitant to switch from Waterfall to Scrum due to concerns over losing control over planning. After training on the flexibility and faster feedback loops that Scrum provides, the team began to see its value.

2. **Start with Small Wins**: Implement Scrum on a small scale, perhaps for a single project or department, to show measurable benefits before rolling it out across the organization. This helps

reduce the fear of change and demonstrates Scrum's value through real-world examples.

- **Tip**: Focus on short sprints to deliver valuable features early, allowing teams to experience the benefits of iterative delivery quickly.

3. **Support from Leadership**: Resistance often stems from uncertainty about whether leadership is fully committed to Scrum. Engage leadership early on, ensuring that they champion the methodology, provide resources, and publicly support the transition.

- **Tip**: Regular **Sprint Reviews** can serve as opportunities for leadership to recognize the team's efforts and reinforce the value of Scrum.

4. **Transparency and Communication**: Clear and consistent communication about the benefits of Scrum helps reduce resistance. Share success stories and explain how Scrum improves project visibility, delivery speed, and customer satisfaction.

- **Example**: A team leader introduces weekly **Q&A sessions** where team members can ask questions about the new process, helping ease concerns.

Managing Time and Resources Effectively

Even the most experienced Scrum teams can struggle with managing time and resources, particularly as startups face shifting priorities and limited resources. Effective management is crucial for staying on track with sprint goals and delivering high-quality work.

Common Time and Resource Management Challenges

1. **Unclear Prioritization**: When priorities change frequently, teams may find themselves stretched thin, working on tasks that don't align with the product vision.

2. **Overcommitment**: Teams often struggle with overcommitting during **Sprint Planning** by accepting more tasks than they can reasonably complete, leading to burnout and decreased morale.

3. **Inefficient Resource Allocation**: Mismanagement of resources, such as not assigning the right people to the right tasks, can slow progress and reduce efficiency.

Strategies for Effective Time and Resource Management

1. **Clear Backlog Prioritization**: The Product Owner plays a key role in ensuring that the **Product Backlog** is clearly prioritized based on business goals. This ensures that the team works on the most critical tasks that deliver value.

    -   **Tip**: Use tools like **Moscow Prioritization** (Must have, Should have, Could have, Won't have) to help structure backlog priorities.

2. **Capacity Planning**: Teams must use historical data, such as **velocity**, to plan their capacity accurately during **Sprint Planning**. Avoid overcommitting by being realistic about what can be achieved within a sprint.

    -   **Example**: A development team has a velocity of 40 story points. During Sprint Planning, they agree to take on no more than 40 points, ensuring they do not overcommit and risk missing sprint goals.

3. **Timeboxing**: Timeboxing is a powerful technique used in Scrum to manage work efficiently. By setting strict time limits for activities like **Daily Stand-ups** (15 minutes) and **Sprint Planning** (no longer than 8 hours for a four-week sprint), teams can ensure they stay focused and productive.

   - **Tip**: Use countdown timers in meetings to reinforce timeboxing and keep discussions concise.

4. **Regular Resource Review**: Regularly review the allocation of resources (team members, tools, etc.) during **Retrospectives** to ensure the right people are working on the right tasks.

   - **Example**: After a Retrospective reveals that too much time is being spent on fixing bugs, the team shifts more resources to quality assurance during the next sprint.

Handling Conflicts Within the Team

Conflicts within a Scrum team can arise due to differences in working styles, personality clashes, or disagreements about the direction of a project. If not managed effectively, these conflicts can derail progress and lower team morale.

Common Sources of Conflict

1. **Differences in Work Styles**: Team members may have different approaches to completing tasks, leading to friction in collaborative efforts.

2. **Role Confusion**: Lack of clarity around the roles of **Product Owner**, **Scrum Master**, and **Development Team** can lead to conflicts over decision-making authority.

3. **Unresolved Tensions**: Small disagreements, if left unresolved, can escalate into bigger conflicts that affect team dynamics.

Strategies for Resolving Conflicts

1. **Open Communication**: Encourage open communication to resolve conflicts early. **Daily Stand-ups** are a good opportunity for team members to voice concerns about progress, workloads, or blockers.

    - **Tip**: Use the **"no-blame" culture** during Retrospectives, where team members discuss issues without attributing fault.

2. **Clear Role Definitions**: Ensure that everyone understands their roles in the team. For example, the Product Owner prioritizes the backlog, the Development Team commits to tasks, and the Scrum Master facilitates the process.

    - **Tip**: Revisit role definitions in Sprint Planning if confusion about decision-making authority arises.

3. **Facilitated Conflict Resolution**: The **Scrum Master** plays a critical role in facilitating conflict resolution. They should mediate discussions, ensure that all perspectives are heard, and guide the team toward a solution.

    - **Example**: A Scrum Master notices tension between the design and development teams over how to implement a feature. They hold a separate session to allow both sides to express concerns and reach a compromise.

4. **Team-building Exercises**: Regular team-building activities can help build trust and reduce conflicts. These exercises encourage

collaboration and help team members better understand each other's strengths and weaknesses.

- **Tip**: Use the end of a **Sprint Retrospective** for a brief team-building activity, such as a problem-solving game, to strengthen bonds and lighten the mood.

Overcoming Product Development Challenges: Addressing the Four Key Risks with Scrum

As startups grow, the complexity of product development increases, often leading to **common challenges** that can derail progress. Among these are four core risks: **value risk**, **usability risk**, **feasibility risk**, and **business viability risk**. These challenges require strategic approaches to ensure that products are not only desirable but also usable, feasible, and sustainable from a business perspective.

1. **Value Risk**: One of the biggest challenges startups face is determining whether they are building the right product. Even a perfectly engineered solution is of no use if it doesn't solve a problem customers care about. In Scrum, this risk is reduced by maintaining an open feedback loop with customers and stakeholders. **Sprint Reviews** at the end of each iteration provide an opportunity to validate that the work completed delivers real value.

   - **Solution**: Regular feedback helps ensure that each sprint delivers meaningful progress and allows teams to pivot quickly if they discover a feature isn't resonating with users.

2. **Usability Risk**: Even if a product solves a real problem, it must also be easy to use. Poor usability can hinder adoption, regardless of the value the product offers. Scrum's short sprints and focus on testing usability early—through user feedback and continuous testing—enable teams to catch and address usability issues long before the product reaches the customer.

   - **Solution**: Usability testing integrated into each sprint ensures that the product is intuitive, minimizing the risk of post-launch frustration from users.

3. **Feasibility Risk**: Often, startups are eager to build ambitious features that push the boundaries of technology. However, many of these features turn out to be unfeasible due to limitations in resources, time, or technical capabilities. Scrum reduces feasibility risk by allowing teams to test and refine the technology in small increments, ensuring that each piece of functionality is technically achievable before moving on to the next.

   - **Solution**: Scrum's iterative model enables early testing of prototypes, ensuring that feasibility challenges are identified and addressed without sinking too many resources into unworkable solutions.

4. **Business Viability Risk**: Finally, it's not enough for a product to be valuable, usable, and feasible—it must also make business sense. Startups face the risk of building products that are not economically viable or scalable. Scrum mitigates this risk by fostering collaboration

between business stakeholders and development teams, ensuring that features align with the company's broader business objectives.

- **Solution**: The constant communication between the Product Owner, stakeholders, and the team ensures that every decision takes into account both product value and business goals.

By tackling these risks head-on with Scrum's transparent and adaptable framework, startups can overcome the most common product development challenges, ensuring that they stay on track and deliver products that are both useful and sustainable.

How Scrum Builds Missionary Teams

One of the deeper cultural shifts that Scrum promotes is the transformation of teams from **mercenaries**—simply delivering tasks without ownership of the product vision—into **missionaries**, who are deeply connected to solving customer problems. This distinction highlights the importance of building teams that are driven by a sense of purpose rather than merely executing tasks. Scrum fosters this **missionary mindset** by empowering teams to take full ownership of their work and encouraging collaboration between cross-functional roles like product managers, designers, and engineers. This approach leads to more innovative solutions and stronger team engagement, essential elements for long-term success in the startup ecosystem.

Case Study: A Scrum Master Resolving Conflicts and Keeping the Team Focused

Case Study: Startup X, a technology startup working on an innovative mobile app, faced internal conflicts that threatened to derail its sprints. The development team often clashed with the Product Owner over priorities, while individual team members had disagreements about the best way to implement features.

Step 1: Addressing Role Confusion

The Scrum Master noticed that many of the conflicts stemmed from confusion over roles, particularly between the Product Owner and the development team. During a **Sprint Retrospective**, the Scrum Master clarified that the Product Owner should prioritize tasks, but the Development Team had autonomy over how to implement them.

Step 2: Facilitating Conflict Resolution

To resolve personal conflicts, the Scrum Master held one-on-one discussions with the involved parties and then facilitated a joint meeting to address the root cause of the tension. By allowing each person to voice their perspective, the team was able to come to an agreement on how to move forward.

Step 3: Refocusing the Team

Once the conflicts were resolved, the Scrum Master refocused the team on the sprint goal, encouraging open communication during **Daily Stand-ups** to prevent further misunderstandings. This helped the team stay on track and meet their sprint commitments.

Outcome:

As a result of the Scrum Master's intervention, Startup X's team became more cohesive and productive. By resolving conflicts early and ensuring clear communication, the team was able to focus on delivering high-quality features without being bogged down by internal disagreements.

Key Takeaways

- Resistance to change is a common obstacle in startups transitioning to Scrum. Addressing concerns early and fostering a culture of transparency helps overcome this resistance.

- Building buy-in from leadership is essential for a smooth Scrum implementation, as top-level support ensures that the team has the resources and time to adapt.

- Time and resource management challenges can be mitigated by using Scrum's iterative approach, focusing on delivering the most valuable features first, and adapting as the project progresses.

- Team conflicts can arise as Scrum teams self-organize and take on new responsibilities. Regular Retrospectives provide a safe space to address issues, improve communication, and build trust.

- Addressing technical debt early prevents future problems and helps maintain the scalability and long-term sustainability of the product.

- Stakeholder engagement is vital for success. Involving stakeholders in Sprint Reviews ensures alignment between the team's work and the organization's goals.

- Scope creep can derail a project's timeline. Maintaining a well-prioritized Product Backlog and focusing on the Sprint Goal helps control scope and ensures the team stays on track.

- Burnout is a risk in fast-paced startups. Scrum's emphasis on sustainable development and regular Retrospectives helps maintain a healthy work-life balance for team members.

- Adaptability and flexibility are key in overcoming challenges in dynamic startup environments. Scrum's iterative approach allows teams to pivot quickly and respond to changing market conditions.

Chapter 9

SMACAR Solutions Case Study

*"Simplicity—the art of maximizing the amount of
work not done—is essential."*

Introduction to SMACAR Solutions

SMACAR Solutions, a startup founded in 2016, embarked on a
mission to integrate Augmented Reality (AR) with Social, Mobile,
Analytics, and Cloud (SMAC) technologies. The company aimed
to revolutionize industries such as retail, real estate, education,
and advertising through cutting-edge AR solutions. As a growing
startup, SMACAR Solutions faced typical challenges such as limited
resources, rapidly evolving technology, and the need for scalability.
Implementing Scrum was pivotal in overcoming these hurdles,
enabling the company to manage its growth from a small team of
three to over 40 employees.

The Need for Scrum at SMACAR Solutions

At its inception, SMACAR Solutions operated with a core
team consisting of the Chief Product Owner (CPO), the Chief
Technology Officer (CTO), and the first developer. The team was
responsible for developing AR prototypes across multiple sectors,

quickly realizing that a structured yet agile approach was necessary to navigate the complexities of product development while remaining adaptable to market demands.

Scrum was chosen as the development framework to:

- Define clear roles and responsibilities for the expanding team.

- Establish a sustainable development pace, especially in the context of deep tech.

- Enhance collaboration and innovation while ensuring transparency and alignment with business goals.

In the short term, SMACAR Solutions focused on developing a Scan and Discovery AR solution using third-party libraries. For long-term scalability, the startup worked toward developing its own proprietary AR algorithm, supported by Scrum's iterative development approach.

Establishing Scrum Roles and Ceremonies

To ensure effective Scrum implementation, SMACAR Solutions appointed two Scrum Masters—one for product development and another for research and development (R&D). The Scrum Master for application development oversaw a cross-functional team that included mobile developers, graphic designers, and web developers, while the Scrum Master for R&D team was responsible for managing interns and fresh graduates skilled in Python and AI/ML libraries like TensorFlow, under the guidance of the CTO.

The team was structured with cross-functional roles, with key responsibilities divided as follows:

- Product Development Team: Tasked with developing the SMACAR AR app and AR Studio.

- R&D Team: Focused on researching and developing proprietary AR algorithms for long-term scalability.

SMACAR Solutions embraced the full range of Scrum ceremonies to maintain development momentum:

- Sprint Planning: Defined the work to be accomplished during two-week sprints, prioritizing user stories that delivered the highest business value.

- Daily Stand-ups: Facilitated communication, allowing team members to address challenges and ensure alignment.

- Sprint Reviews: Presented completed work to stakeholders, enabling feedback that was integrated into the Product Backlog.

- Sprint Retrospectives: Encouraged continuous improvement by reflecting on successes and challenges from each sprint.

Definition of Ready (DoR): Setting the Stage for Success

While Scrum formally emphasizes the **Definition of Done (DoD)**, the **Definition of Ready (DoR)** plays an equally vital role by ensuring that Product Backlog Items (PBIs) are fully prepared and actionable before entering a sprint. The DoR and DoD serve distinct but complementary functions in Scrum:

- **Definition of Ready (DoR)**: Determines when a backlog item is prepared for the team to start work. A PBI meets the DoR when it has clear requirements, acceptance criteria, supporting documentation, and estimated effort, enabling the team to take action confidently.

- **Definition of Done (DoD)**: Indicates when a task or PBI is fully complete, meeting quality standards and potentially ready for release.

At **SMACAR Solutions**, adhering to a DoR was essential to maintain a smooth workflow and minimize uncertainty. Each PBI had to meet specific DoR criteria before entering a sprint:

- **Clear Acceptance Criteria**: Detailed criteria outlined what needed to be achieved for completion.

- **Supporting Documentation**: Requirements, wireframes, and data were attached to each PBI, avoiding last-minute questions.

- **Stakeholder Approval**: All PBIs were reviewed and approved by stakeholders, ensuring alignment with business goals.

- **Effort Estimation**: Techniques like Planning Poker allowed the team to assess and align effort estimates with sprint goals.

By differentiating between the DoR and DoD, SMACAR Solutions ensured that each sprint began with **well-prepared items** and concluded with **high-quality, complete**

deliverables. This approach helped reinforce accountability and supported a culture of continuous improvement, enhancing SMACAR Solutions' overall Scrum process.

Challenges and Adaptation

Despite the structured approach provided by Scrum, the team at SMACAR Solutions encountered several challenges:

- A number of team members were new to Agile methodologies, which required additional time and effort to adapt to Scrum practices.

- Working within a deep tech industry, the team needed to remain up-to-date with rapidly changing technologies, particularly in AR.

- Securing buy-in from stakeholders proved challenging, as many investors were unfamiliar with Scrum and initially skeptical of its benefits.

- Unclear client requirements at times slowed progress, leading to multiple iterations before reaching final agreements.

- Talent acquisition was difficult due to budget constraints, requiring the company to cultivate a collaborative culture to retain key employees.

Despite these hurdles, SMACAR Solutions persevered, continuously adapting its Scrum practices and building a strong Agile culture within the organization. Key Agile principles such as transparency, inspection, and adaptation were instrumental in fostering a team environment where innovation could thrive.

Successes and Key Outcomes

Over time, Scrum became an integral part of SMACAR Solutions' culture. The following key outcomes illustrate the impact of Scrum on the startup's growth:

- Cross-functional collaboration significantly improved, with well-defined roles and responsibilities across product development and R&D teams.

- The SMACAR AR App and AR Studio were developed and launched within six months, enabling users to scan printed materials and view digital content. The iterative approach enabled rapid feature releases.

- Within 18 months, the SMACAR AR app garnered more than 10,000 downloads and attracted over 200 studio users, with 20+ custom client implementations worldwide.

- SMACAR Solutions scaled its team from three to over 40 members, utilizing Scrum of Scrums to manage multiple teams and maintain coordination across product development and R&D efforts.

Lessons Learned

SMACAR Solutions' journey with Scrum highlighted several key lessons for other startups:

1. Leadership and a clear product vision are critical to maintaining alignment across the team.

2. Adaptability is essential: The startup continuously refined its Scrum processes to align with its growth and the evolving needs of the market.

3. Fostering team culture is vital for success. SMACAR Solutions emphasized the Scrum values of Focus, Respect, Openness, Courage, and Commitment, creating an environment of trust and collaboration.

4. Scaling Scrum requires careful planning and execution. By adopting Scrum of Scrums, SMACAR Solutions ensured that teams remained aligned while maintaining agility.

5. Client feedback proved invaluable in product development, with frequent feedback loops allowing the team to refine the product and ensure it met user needs.

Key Takeaways

- Scrum provided structure and flexibility, enabling SMACAR Solutions to manage the complexities of developing innovative AR solutions while adapting to rapidly evolving technologies.

- Cross-functional collaboration was a key factor in the success of SMACAR Solutions, with teams structured around well-defined roles and responsibilities in both product development and R&D.

- Scrum ceremonies like Sprint Planning, Daily Stand-ups, Sprint Reviews, and Retrospectives helped the team stay aligned and continuously improve, even in a deep-tech startup environment.

- Scaling Scrum was successfully achieved through the adoption of Scrum of Scrums, allowing the company to coordinate efforts across multiple teams and maintain agility as the team grew from three to over 40 members.

- Client feedback played a pivotal role in the product development cycle, with regular Sprint Reviews ensuring that SMACAR Solutions' AR products were aligned with customer needs.

- Despite challenges such as resistance to Agile from stakeholders and talent acquisition hurdles, the team adapted and thrived by fostering a strong Agile culture built on the Scrum values of Focus, Respect, Openness, Courage, and Commitment.

- The iterative nature of Scrum enabled the successful launch of the SMACAR AR App and AR Studio within six months, achieving rapid growth with more than 10,000 downloads and over 200 studio users.

- Lessons learned from the SMACAR Solutions experience highlight the importance of strong leadership, adaptability, and the ability to scale Scrum effectively as the team and product portfolio grow.

Chapter 10

Future of Scrum in Startups

*"The best architectures, requirements, and designs
emerge from self-organizing teams."*

As the startup ecosystem continues to evolve, so does the way teams operate and manage their workflows. Scrum, as a dominant framework in agile project management, has proven itself time and time again as a valuable tool for startups looking to scale, innovate, and remain adaptable in fast-changing markets. But what does the future hold for Scrum? In this chapter, we will explore emerging trends, innovations in Agile practices, the potential for Scrum across various industries, and how Scrum may evolve to meet the unique challenges startups will face in the coming years.

Trends and Innovations in Agile Practices

Scrum, like all Agile frameworks, must continuously adapt to changes in technology, market conditions, and the expectations of startup teams. Several trends and innovations are emerging that will likely shape how Scrum evolves.

1. Hybrid Agile Frameworks

In the past few years, there has been a growing trend of blending Scrum with other Agile frameworks such as **Kanban**, **Lean**, and **Extreme Programming (XP)**. These hybrid approaches allow teams to adapt Scrum's iterative nature while leveraging the strengths of other methodologies to meet the specific needs of their startups.

- **ScrumBan**: One example is **ScrumBan**, a hybrid that combines Scrum's sprint structure with Kanban's continuous flow model. Startups using ScrumBan benefit from Scrum's structure while maintaining Kanban's flexibility for handling unplanned work. This approach works well for teams that need to juggle both project-based work and ongoing operational tasks.

- **Lean-Agile Approaches**: The fusion of **Lean** principles with Scrum helps teams eliminate waste, improve efficiency, and focus on delivering maximum value with minimal resources. Lean-Agile practices will likely continue to gain traction as startups strive to be more resource-efficient.

Scrum vs. Kanban: A Quick Comparison		
Aspect	**Scrum**	**Kanban**
Purpose	Framework for structured, iterative work in short, time-boxed sprints	Visual workflow management method for continuous delivery without fixed iterations

Aspect	Scrum	Kanban
Roles	Defined roles: **Product Owner, Scrum Master, Development Team**	No fixed roles; team members may take on multiple roles as needed
Iterations	Time-boxed sprints, typically 1-4 weeks	No time-boxed sprints; work is continuously pulled from the backlog based on capacity
Planning	Sprint Planning meeting at the start of each sprint	No formal planning meeting; backlog items are added as needed
Work Limitation	Work is planned at the beginning of each sprint and cannot be changed during the sprint	Work-in-Progress (WIP) limits are set per workflow stage to control task flow
Meetings/ Ceremonies	Structured ceremonies: Sprint Planning, Daily Stand-ups, Sprint Review, and Retrospective	No required meetings; may have ad-hoc reviews or stand-ups as needed

Aspect	Scrum	Kanban
Focus	The team commits to a set amount of work to be completed within the sprint.	Emphasis on maximizing workflow efficiency by managing WIP and reducing cycle time
Metrics	Velocity (average story points per sprint), burndown charts for tracking sprint progress	Cycle time (time taken to complete a task) and throughput for tracking task completion rate
Flexibility	Limited changes are allowed within a sprint	High flexibility; tasks can be reprioritized anytime
Best Use Case	Ideal for complex projects requiring iterative work and time-boxed deliverables	Suited for continuous-flow projects where tasks vary in size and priority

Scrum and **Kanban** each offer distinct advantages for managing workflows and achieving efficiency in startups. Scrum, with its structured framework and time-boxed sprints, is well-suited for projects with evolving requirements and well-defined stages of work. Teams working with Scrum benefit from regular feedback cycles and a clear cadence of ceremonies, making it an ideal choice for startups that need to iterate rapidly on product features while managing stakeholder expectations.

Kanban, on the other hand, is optimal for teams that prioritize workflow continuity and need to balance diverse tasks without fixed time constraints. Its flexibility makes it effective in environments where priorities shift frequently, allowing teams to focus on reducing task cycle times and managing WIP limits. Unlike Scrum, Kanban does not prescribe a fixed process, enabling each team to adapt the system based on unique needs and bottlenecks.

Real-World Example of Kanban in R&D: Huawei

Huawei, the global telecommunications and technology giant, utilizes Kanban within its **R&D departments** to manage complex projects and streamline its research initiatives. Given Huawei's focus on **cutting-edge technology**—from telecommunications to artificial intelligence—its R&D teams handle diverse, unpredictable tasks that require flexibility. By adopting Kanban, Huawei has been able to manage **multiple research streams** effectively, setting Work-in-Progress (WIP) limits to control task load, minimize bottlenecks, and ensure steady progress across different R&D functions.

Kanban enables Huawei's R&D teams to quickly pivot as new data or research findings emerge, allowing for real-time adjustments in priority and resource allocation. This approach has proven particularly valuable in **deep tech** fields like **5G** and **AI**, where timelines and requirements are often fluid, and rapid iterations are necessary. With Kanban, Huawei achieves both **agility and control**, making it possible to bring innovative products to market while continuously refining its technology through adaptive R&D workflows.

2. DevOps Integration with Scrum

Another growing trend is the integration of **DevOps** with Scrum to enhance collaboration between development and operations teams. The traditional separation between these two functions can create bottlenecks in software deployment, which is why more startups are adopting **Agile-DevOps** approaches. By incorporating continuous integration, continuous delivery (CI/CD), and automated testing into the Scrum framework, teams can speed up the release cycle while maintaining high-quality standards.

- **Continuous Deployment**: DevOps practices like continuous deployment enable startups to release features faster and with more reliability. Combining this with Scrum's focus on iterative improvement helps startups adapt to user feedback more quickly and keep pace with market demands.

- **Automation in Scrum**: Automation tools for testing, integration, and deployment are becoming more common, allowing Scrum teams to minimize manual processes and increase the speed of delivery. This trend is especially valuable for tech startups looking to scale quickly while maintaining Agile flexibility.

3. Remote and Distributed Scrum Teams

The shift toward remote and distributed work, accelerated by the global pandemic, is also shaping the future of Scrum. Tools like

Zoom, **Slack**, **Miro**, and **Jira** have become essential for managing remote Scrum teams. As remote work becomes more normalized, Scrum will need to continue evolving to accommodate fully distributed teams while ensuring collaboration and communication remain seamless.

- **Asynchronous Scrum**: Distributed teams across different time zones are increasingly adopting **asynchronous Scrum** practices. This allows teams to manage Daily Stand-ups, Sprint Planning, and reviews without needing all team members online simultaneously, making Scrum more adaptable for global startups.

- **Virtual Collaboration Tools**: The use of digital whiteboards, task management tools, and other online collaboration platforms will remain crucial for keeping Scrum ceremonies productive in a remote-first world. Innovations in these tools will likely enhance the way Scrum teams operate.

4. AI and Machine Learning in Agile

Artificial intelligence (AI) and machine learning (ML) are beginning to play a role in how teams manage workflows and make decisions in Scrum. AI-driven tools can assist teams in predicting sprint velocity, automating routine tasks, and even suggesting improvements based on data analytics.

- **AI for Sprint Planning**: AI tools can analyze historical data to predict the optimal number of tasks a team can complete in a sprint, making Sprint Planning more accurate.

- **Automation of Metrics**: ML algorithms can help automate the generation of Agile metrics like velocity, cycle time, and defect rates, providing teams with real-time insights into their performance.

Potential for Scrum in Various Startup Industries

Scrum has traditionally been most popular in software development, but its application is expanding to other industries. Startups in sectors such as healthcare, education, FinTech, and manufacturing are beginning to adopt Scrum to address their specific challenges.

1. Healthcare Startups

In the healthcare industry, where compliance and regulatory standards are critical, Scrum is gaining traction as a tool for building adaptive, patient-centric solutions. Healthcare startups are leveraging Scrum's flexibility to iterate quickly on healthcare software, devices, and systems while ensuring compliance with regulations.

- **Example**: Startups working on telemedicine platforms or health management apps use Scrum to quickly deliver updates based on patient feedback, improving the user experience while staying compliant with healthcare regulations.

2. FinTech Startups

The fast-paced world of FinTech startups demands agility in response to evolving regulatory landscapes, security needs, and customer demands. Scrum is widely adopted by FinTech startups to rapidly build and deploy new features, allowing them to stay ahead of the competition while maintaining high levels of security.

- **Example**: Scrum helps FinTech startups like mobile banking and payment platforms stay nimble as they develop new features in response to regulatory changes and customer needs for secure, fast transactions.

3. Education Startups (EdTech)

The rise of **EdTech** has made Scrum a popular framework for startups looking to rapidly build and iterate on online learning platforms. Agile approaches help education startups manage complex projects involving educators, students, and institutional stakeholders.

- **Example**: Education startups use Scrum to prioritize feature development based on feedback from students and teachers, ensuring that online learning platforms remain engaging and relevant.

4. Manufacturing and Hardware Startups

Even in industries traditionally resistant to Agile practices, like hardware and manufacturing, Scrum is finding a foothold. By applying Scrum principles to product development and prototyping, manufacturing startups can bring new products to market faster and more efficiently.

- **Example**: Hardware startups use Scrum to prototype devices in short cycles, gather customer feedback early, and refine their designs before moving to mass production.

Vision for the Future of Scrum in the Startup Ecosystem

As we look to the future, the role of Scrum in the startup ecosystem will continue to grow and evolve, adapting to new challenges, technologies, and business models. Here are some key areas where Scrum is poised to make a significant impact:

1. Scrum Beyond Software

While Scrum was originally designed for software development, its principles of iterative work, team collaboration, and continuous improvement are increasingly being applied to non-technical teams, such as marketing, HR, and finance. The future of Scrum may see broader adoption in these non-technical areas of startups, where agility and adaptability are becoming just as important as in tech teams.

- **Example**: Marketing teams in startups are beginning to adopt Scrum to plan and execute campaigns iteratively, allowing for faster adjustments based on real-time data and customer feedback.

2. Scaling Scrum for Enterprise Startups

As startups grow into larger enterprises, scaling Scrum across multiple teams becomes more challenging. **Scaling frameworks** like **SAFe (Scaled Agile Framework)**, **LeSS (Large-Scale Scrum)**, and **Scrum@Scale** are emerging to address these challenges. The future of Scrum will likely involve more widespread adoption of these scaling frameworks to help larger startups and enterprises maintain agility as they expand.

- **Example**: A fast-growing SaaS startup may use **SAFe** to align multiple Scrum teams working on different parts of the product, ensuring that all teams stay coordinated as they scale.

3. Focus on Sustainable Practices

As sustainability becomes a critical focus for startups, Scrum teams will likely adopt more environmentally conscious practices. This could involve using Scrum to streamline processes that reduce waste, optimize resource usage, and ensure that startups contribute positively to environmental goals.

- **Example**: A startup focused on sustainability might use Scrum to continuously iterate on ways to reduce their carbon footprint, improve product sustainability, or streamline supply chain processes.

4. Scrum and Agile Leadership

As Scrum evolves, the role of **Agile leadership** will become even more critical. Scrum Masters and Product Owners will be expected to not only facilitate the Scrum process but also act as agile leaders, fostering innovation, driving change, and building cultures of continuous improvement. In the future, Scrum leadership roles may expand to include more strategic responsibilities, such as guiding the product vision or influencing organizational agility beyond the development team.

Case Study: TechVision – Leveraging AI for Agile Workflow Enhancement

TechVision, a growing AI-powered startup building digital solutions for e-commerce platforms, recognized that their development and product management teams were spending significant time on repetitive tasks, such as generating user stories, estimating work, and forecasting sprints. They decided to experiment with incorporating **Generative AI** and other AI-driven tools to optimize their Scrum process, reduce time spent on routine tasks, and improve Sprint Planning accuracy.

The AI-Driven Transformation

TechVision introduced AI-driven tools into their Scrum framework, including generative AI models like **GPT** for user story creation, machine learning algorithms for forecasting sprint velocity, and automated project management tools for real-time backlog prioritization.

- **Generating User Stories with AI**: One of the first challenges TechVision faced was the amount of time product owners and team members spent writing detailed user stories. By integrating a generative AI tool (similar to GPT), the team was able to input basic requirements or feature ideas, and the AI generated user stories in a structured format. This significantly reduced the time spent on drafting stories while maintaining quality.

  - **Example**: A simple prompt such as "As a customer, I want to easily track my order status" would be expanded by the AI into a fully fleshed-out user story, complete with acceptance criteria and potential edge cases. This allowed the Product Owner to quickly review and prioritize stories in the backlog.

- **Sprint Forecasting with Machine Learning**: TechVision also employed **machine learning** models to forecast the velocity of upcoming sprints based on historical data. By analyzing past sprint performance, the AI could predict the team's likely output in terms of story points, helping the Scrum Master and Product Owner make more informed decisions during Sprint Planning.

  - **Example**: Based on previous sprints, the AI forecasted that the team could comfortably handle 35 story points in the upcoming sprint. This allowed the team to avoid overcommitting, improving sprint outcomes.

- **AI-Driven Backlog Prioritization**: TechVision leveraged AI algorithms to help prioritize their Product Backlog. The AI analyzed metrics such as user engagement, market trends, and customer feedback to recommend the most impactful features for the next sprint. This helped the team focus on the highest-value tasks that would deliver measurable benefits to their users.

  - **Example**: The AI identified that certain features related to customer engagement had the highest potential for increasing user retention. The Product Owner used these insights to prioritize those features for the next sprint.

Results and Best Practices

1. **Increased Efficiency in Sprint Planning**: By using AI to automate user story creation and sprint forecasting, the team reduced the time spent on Sprint Planning sessions by 30%. This freed up more time for team members to focus on actual development work.

2. **Improved Forecast Accuracy**: Machine learning-based velocity forecasts led to more accurate Sprint Planning, with TechVision's sprint success rate improving by 25% as the team made more realistic commitments based on data-driven predictions.

3. **Faster Backlog Refinement**: AI-driven backlog prioritization allowed the Product Owner to make more informed decisions about which features to prioritize. This resulted in a 20% increase in customer satisfaction, as the team focused on features that directly addressed user needs.

Lessons Learned

- **AI Complements, Not Replaces**: While AI tools significantly reduced manual work and improved decision-making, TechVision found that human oversight remained critical. Product Owners and Scrum Masters still needed to validate AI-generated user stories and ensure that backlog priorities aligned with broader business goals.

- **Continuous Improvement**: By regularly evaluating the AI's performance in generating user stories and forecasts, TechVision was able to refine how they used the technology, continuously improving the quality of output over time.

Key Takeaways

- Hybrid Agile frameworks, such as ScrumBan and Lean-Agile, are gaining popularity, combining Scrum's structure with flexibility from Kanban and Lean principles to meet evolving startup needs.

- DevOps integration with Scrum helps startups streamline continuous integration and deployment (CI/CD), enabling faster feature releases and more reliable product development cycles.

- Remote and distributed Scrum teams are becoming the norm, with tools like Zoom, Slack, and Miro supporting global collaboration, and asynchronous practices emerging to accommodate different time zones.

- AI and machine learning are playing a growing role in Scrum workflows, improving Sprint Planning accuracy, automating backlog prioritization, and providing real-time performance metrics through predictive analytics.

- Scrum is expanding beyond software development into industries such as healthcare, FinTech, education (EdTech), and manufacturing, where agility is critical to product development and compliance.

- Healthcare startups use Scrum to iterate quickly on patient-centric solutions while maintaining compliance with stringent regulatory standards.

- FinTech startups benefit from Scrum's flexibility in responding to regulatory changes and delivering secure, fast features for users.

- Manufacturing startups are using Scrum for prototyping and refining hardware designs, allowing them to gather feedback earlier and bring products to market faster.

- Scrum beyond software: Scrum principles are increasingly being applied to non-technical teams, including marketing, HR, and finance, where iterative work and team collaboration are crucial for achieving business goals.

- The future of Scrum will involve greater adoption of scaling frameworks for startups growing into larger enterprises, ensuring agility is maintained as teams and products expand.

Conclusion:
Embracing Scrum for Startup Success

"At regular intervals, the team reflects on how to become more effective, then tunes and adjusts its behavior accordingly."

As we've explored throughout this book, Scrum offers a dynamic and adaptive framework that allows startups to navigate uncertainty, manage their workflows effectively, and accelerate innovation. This journey through Scrum has touched on every aspect of startup growth, from understanding the basics of Agile practices to implementing Scrum at scale and continuously improving through feedback loops. Let's revisit some of the key takeaways from each chapter and explore the resources that will help you take your Scrum practice even further.

Recap of Key Chapters

1. **Introduction to Scrum**: We started by understanding how Scrum, as a flexible and iterative framework, helps startups manage their workflows, foster collaboration, and ensure continuous improvement. The focus was on how Scrum can

help startups be more adaptable and customer-centric in their approach.

2. **Scrum Basics**: In Chapter 1, we covered the essential principles of Scrum, such as its foundation in empiricism, transparency, and accountability. By implementing the core ceremonies—Sprint Planning, Daily Stand-ups, Sprint Reviews, and Retrospectives—teams can stay aligned and adaptable.

3. **Setting Up Scrum in a Startup**: Here, we examined how startups can prepare their teams and environment to embrace Scrum. From building a Scrum board to assigning roles like the Product Owner, Scrum Master, and Development Team, this chapter emphasized the importance of setting the foundation for a successful Scrum journey.

4. **Product Backlog Management**: In this chapter, we discussed the importance of creating, prioritizing, and refining the Product Backlog. We explored how effective user stories and backlog grooming help teams stay focused on delivering value to customers.

5. **Scaling Scrum**: As your startup grows, so do the challenges of scaling Scrum. Chapter 5 explored frameworks like Scrum of Scrums, SAFe, and LeSS, offering solutions to manage multiple Scrum teams working together seamlessly.

6. **Enhancing Team Collaboration**: Chapter 6 emphasized the importance of building a collaborative culture, implementing effective communication strategies, and leveraging the right tools, particularly for remote teams.

7. **Measuring Success**: We explored the metrics that matter most for Scrum teams, including velocity, burndown charts,

and cycle time. We also discussed how to drive continuous improvement through Retrospectives.

8. **Overcoming Challenges**: Whether it's addressing resistance to change, managing time and resources, or resolving conflicts, Chapter 8 provided actionable solutions to some of the most common obstacles Scrum teams face.

9. **SMACAR Solutions Case Study**: Chapter 9 highlighted the real-world example of a startup that successfully implemented Scrum, showing how Agile practices can help deliver value faster, improve product quality, and foster innovation.

10. **The Future of Scrum**: Finally, in Chapter 10, we looked ahead to how trends like hybrid Agile frameworks, DevOps integration, and AI-driven advancements will shape the future of Scrum in startups.

Encouragement to Adopt Scrum in Startups

Scrum is more than just a framework; it's a mindset that fosters continuous improvement, collaboration and agility. Whether your startup is at an early stage or scaling rapidly, Scrum provides a structured yet flexible approach to handling complex projects, delivering value iteratively and responding to customer feedback quickly.

By adopting Scrum, your startup can:

- **Deliver high-quality products faster** by breaking down work into smaller, manageable pieces.

- **Adapt to changing market demands** with the ability to pivot based on real-time feedback.

- **Foster a culture of continuous learning** where teams improve incrementally with each sprint.

If you're serious about bringing Scrum to your startup, now is the time to act. Get your teams trained, set up Scrum boards, and start small—implementing Scrum for one project or department— and expand as you gain momentum.

Resources for Further Exploration

To continue your Scrum journey, consider the following resources. These include books, courses, and communities that will help deepen your understanding of Scrum and Agile practices, while also providing opportunities to connect with like-minded professionals.

Scrum Alliance

- **Website**: scrumalliance.org

- **What It Offers**: Scrum Alliance is a leading organization in the Scrum community, offering certifications, resources, and access to a global network of Scrum practitioners.

- **Certifications**:

  - **Certified ScrumMaster (CSM)**: Ideal for anyone looking to lead Scrum teams and facilitate Scrum practices.

  - **Certified Scrum Product Owner (CSPO)**: Aimed at product managers and owners responsible for backlog management and value delivery.

  - **Advanced Certifications**: For experienced professionals, advanced certifications like the **Certified Scrum**

Professional (CSP) and **Agile Coaching** credentials are available.

- **Why It's Useful**: Scrum Alliance offers comprehensive learning paths, helping professionals deepen their knowledge of Scrum and Agile leadership.

Evelyn Konsult

- **Website**: evelynkonsult.se

- **What It Offers**: Evelyn Konsult, led by thought leader **Evelyn Tian**, provides an array of Agile and Scrum training programs designed to elevate product leadership, Agile coaching, and Scrum mastery. With options for certification via **Scrum Alliance** and **ICF**, the platform offers both paid and free learning opportunities through interactive cohort setups.

- **Resources**:

  - **Coaching Circles**: Free coaching circles for discussing Agile leadership and Scrum practices with a global community.

  - **Certifications**: Certifications for **Certified ScrumMaster (CSM)**, **Certified Scrum Product Owner (CSPO)**, and Agile leadership.

- **Why It's Useful**: Evelyn Konsult's focus on mentorship, coupled with the diverse global community, makes it a great resource for both new and experienced professionals looking to grow in Agile leadership and coaching roles.

Leanpitch

- **Website**: leanpitch.com

- **What It Offers**: Leanpitch specializes in experiential learning through **Scrum** and **Agile coaching** certifications. They offer certifications for Scrum Masters, Agile Coaches, and Product Owners, with a hands-on approach that bridges theory and real-world application.

- **Resources**:

    - **Role-Based Learning**: Learning paths tailored to specific Agile roles like **Scrum Master**, **Product Owner**, and **Agile Coach**.

    - **Workshops**: In-depth workshops that combine Agile principles with leadership and coaching skills.

- **Why It's Useful**: Leanpitch's focus on role-based learning paths and practical workshops makes it ideal for those looking to deeply engage with their Agile roles, ensuring both professional growth and real-world applicability.

KnowledgeHut

- **Website**: knowledgehut.com

- **What It Offers**: KnowledgeHut is a global provider of Agile and Scrum training, offering certifications ranging from beginner to advanced levels. Their programs cover **Certified ScrumMaster (CSM)**, **Certified Scrum Product Owner (CSPO)**, and **Certified Agile Leadership (CAL)**, blending theory with practice to drive Agile transformations.

- **Resources**:

  - **Virtual Courses**: Interactive virtual courses that provide hands-on mentorship and real-time feedback.

  - **Workshops**: Specialized Agile workshops, including topics on **Scrum**, **Kanban**, and integrating Agile with emerging technologies like **DevOps**.

- **Why It's Useful**: KnowledgeHut offers a wide range of Agile courses, backed by an engaging virtual platform that ensures a well-rounded learning experience. Their focus on emerging technologies and Agile integration makes them an excellent resource for professionals looking to stay ahead in the Agile field.

Silicon Valley Product Group (SVPG)

- **Website**: svpg.com

- **What It Offers**: SVPG, founded by Marty Cagan, is a hub for product managers and leaders who want to build great products using Agile and Scrum practices. SVPG offers insights into product strategy, user-centered design, and empowered teams.

- **Resources**:

  - **Articles**: A comprehensive library of articles on product development, leadership, and agile practices.

  - **Workshops**: In-depth workshops on building empowered product teams and aligning product strategy with Agile practices.

- **Why It's Useful**: SVPG's insights into product strategy and team empowerment complement Scrum practices, helping startups build agile teams focused on delivering user value.

These resources will empower you to not only deepen your knowledge of Agile practices but also join a global network of professionals dedicated to driving innovation and continuous improvement through Scrum. Whether you're just starting out or looking to advance your career, these platforms offer a wealth of knowledge to help you along your Agile journey.

Books

- **"Scrum: The Art of Doing Twice the Work in Half the Time"** by **Jeff Sutherland**

  This foundational book explains the core principles of Scrum and provides real-world examples of how Scrum can transform teams to deliver more efficiently and effectively.

- **"Inspired: How to Create Products Customers Love"** by **Marty Cagan**

  Focused on product management, this book is ideal for product managers seeking to integrate Agile development principles with Scrum to build customer-centric products.

- **"The Lean Startup: How Today's Entrepreneurs Use Continuous Innovation to Create Radically Successful Businesses"** by **Eric Ries**

  While not specific to Scrum, this book complements Agile practices by focusing on iterative product development, customer feedback loops, and lean processes that startups can use to stay adaptable.

- **"Agile Estimating and Planning"** by **Mike Cohn**

  A go-to resource for learning how to effectively estimate and plan in Agile environments, covering topics like user stories, velocity, and release planning.

- **"Essential Scrum: A Practical Guide to the Most Popular Agile Process"** by **Kenneth S. Rubin**

  This book is perfect for anyone looking to understand the practical applications of Scrum, covering everything from Scrum roles to meetings and artifacts, with real-world examples.

- **"Scrum and XP from the Trenches"** by **Henrik Kniberg**

  This book offers a hands-on look at how to implement Scrum and **Extreme Programming (XP)** together. It's highly practical and based on Kniberg's experience leading Scrum teams.

- **"The Phoenix Project: A Novel About IT, DevOps, and Helping Your Business Win"** by **Gene Kim, Kevin Behr, and George Spafford**

  While not a direct Scrum book, this novel gives powerful insights into how Agile practices, including Scrum and DevOps, can help turn failing projects around.

- **"Kanban: Successful Evolutionary Change for Your Technology Business"** by **David J. Anderson**

  This book is excellent for understanding how Kanban can complement or evolve from Scrum practices. It's especially useful for teams managing workflow and prioritizing tasks dynamically.

- **"The Five Dysfunctions of a Team: A Leadership Fable"** by **Patrick Lencioni**

  Though not Scrum-specific, this book delves into team dynamics, offering valuable insights for Scrum Masters and team leaders on how to build cohesive, high-performing teams.

- **"User Story Mapping: Discover the Whole Story, Build the Right Product"** by **Jeff Patton**

  This book focuses on how to use **user story mapping** in Agile environments to ensure the right product gets built through collaborative planning and iterative development.

This list of books provides a comprehensive mix of Scrum, Agile methodologies, team management, and product development principles, helping your readers deepen their understanding of how Agile and Scrum work in different contexts.

A Final Word

Scrum is a powerful tool for driving innovation, efficiency, and collaboration in startups. As your startup grows, embracing Scrum will help you navigate complexity, deliver high-quality products, and maintain your competitive edge. By taking advantage of the wealth of resources available—whether it's the insights from SVPG, certifications from Scrum Alliance, or the wealth of books and courses—you can continue to refine your Scrum practices and lead your teams to success.

In the end, Scrum is about empowering teams to continuously improve and adapt. It's not just a framework but a way of thinking that allows startups to remain agile, focus on value, and grow sustainably. Embrace it, evolve with it, and watch your startup thrive.

References

1. "Scrum: The Art of Doing Twice the Work in Half the Time" by Jeff Sutherland

2. "The Scrum Guide" by Ken Schwaber and Jeff Sutherland

3. "Inspired: How to Create Products Customers Love" by Marty Cagan

4. Scrum Alliance (Website): scrumalliance.org

5. Silicon Valley Product Group (SVPG) (Website): svpg.com

6. "Agile Estimating and Planning" by Mike Cohn

7. "The Lean Startup" by Eric Ries

8. "Essential Scrum: A Practical Guide to the Most Popular Agile Process" by Kenneth S. Rubin

9. Scaled Agile Framework (SAFe) (Website): scaledagileframework.com

10. Large Scale Scrum (LeSS) (Website): less.works

11. "Scrum and XP from the Trenches" by Henrik Kniberg

12. "The Agile Manifesto" agilemanifesto.org

13. Scrum.org (Website): scrum.org

14. "Agile Project Management with Scrum" by Ken Schwaber

15. Mountain Goat Software (Website): mountaingoatsoftware.com

16. "The Phoenix Project: A Novel About IT, DevOps, and Helping Your Business Win" by Gene Kim, Kevin Behr, and George Spafford

17. Scaled Agile, Inc. (Website): scaledagile.com

18. Atlassian (Website): atlassian.com

19. "The Elements of Scrum" by Chris Sims and Hillary Louise Johnson

20. "Kanban: Successful Evolutionary Change for Your Technology Business" by David J. Anderson

21. Agile Alliance (Website): agilealliance.org

22. Agile Coaching Institute (Website): agilecoachinginstitute.com

About the Author

Sreehari Unnikrishnan (Harry Unni) is a seasoned Agile and product management professional with over two decades of IT experience spanning industries such as hospitality, healthcare, consumer products, and emerging technologies like AI, Augmented Reality (AR), and Virtual Reality (VR). His career is built on a deep understanding of Agile methodologies, with a particular focus on Scrum and its ability to empower teams to achieve their best work.

Harry's journey in Agile formally began in 2011, and since then he has played key roles as a Scrum Master, Product Owner, and Agile Coach, driving numerous Agile transformations. His reputation for building high-performing teams is underscored by his commitment to fostering collaboration and transparency within organizations. Those who have worked with Harry often describe him as a visionary leader—someone who brings both technical expertise and a deep passion for empowering teams to succeed. Colleagues frequently highlight his ability to simplify complex concepts, making Agile accessible to teams at all levels.

As the co-founder and director of SMACAR Solutions, Harry led the development of innovative Augmented Reality products for clients in retail and e-commerce. Under his guidance, the company implemented Scrum for product development and R&D efforts, enabling rapid iterations and continuous feedback from clients while fostering a culture of continuous improvement.

Beyond his hands-on work with startups, Harry has a strong foundation in academia. During his MBA, he published the research paper "Extending Technology Adoption Model by Addition of Cognitive Inhibitors," which provided fresh insights into how organizations can better manage the adoption of new technologies. This academic exploration complements his practical experience, informing his approach to leading Agile transformations and guiding companies toward sustainable growth.

Throughout his career, Harry has been lauded for his strategic mindset and collaborative spirit, often receiving praise for his ability to motivate and inspire teams to exceed their potential. His colleagues describe him as someone who brings both humility and confidence to leadership, always open to learning while providing clear, decisive guidance when needed.

The tagline "Do To Know To Know To Do," a palindrome sentence, best describes his mindset to constantly "learn by doing" as he continues to explore new technologies and Agile practices, always seeking ways to bring innovation and agility into the organizations he works with. His passion for Scrum and Agile is not just about process—it's about empowering teams to be more creative, adaptive, and successful in an ever-changing business landscape.